Bicycling Books®

BASIC BICYCLE REPAIR

by the editors of ***Bicycling***® magazine

Printed in the United States of America on recycled paper, containing a high percentage of de-inked fiber.

Cover photograph by Margaret Smyser

Book series design by K. A. Schell

Layout by Jeanne Stock

Illustrations by David Bullock

Library of Congress Catologing in Publication Data

Main entry under title:

Basic bicycle repair.

(Bicycling books series)
1. Bicycles—Maintenance and repair.
I. Bicycling (Emmaus, Pa.) II. Series.
TL430.B37 629.28′772 80–21859
ISBN 0-87857-315-1 paperback
10 paperback

Contents

Introduction

Recently John Rakowski, world bicycle traveler, stopped by the offices of *Bicycling* magazine. He had just returned from a 5,000-mile jaunt through northern Europe. His conversation was about the land, the people, and the haunting quiet of the open road.

He didn't talk about bike repair. He did mention in passing that he didn't experience one flat tire during his trip, which he attributed to equipment choice, riding techniques, and a good bit of luck.

On the other hand, I know a number of people who suffer more than their share of flats and other problems within a square mile of their homes.

More frequently, people are reluctant to travel more than a stone's throw from a fixed departure point because they are afraid of mechanical breakdown. They ask themselves: what would I do if I got a flat tire or if a spoke on the freewheel side broke?

These are legitimate questions and must be answered satisfactorily if someone is to use the bicycle as an alternate form of transportation. And the point is that anyone, no matter his or her mechanical inclinations, can learn enough about basic bicycle repair to be liberated from worries about the consequences of a flat tire or brake failure.

This book should amply fulfill that need. It is prepared by the editors of *Bicycling* magazine who, through much experience, have mastered the art of efficient bicycle repair. Specifically, *Basic Bicycle Repair* starts you off on the right foot by providing all the essential information about tools that you'll be likely to need for any on- or off-road repair.

Keeping in mind that most bike repairs are relatively simple, the contributors have given good emphasis to certain problem areas, including gears, brakes, and tires. Once you master these areas, you'll be more than prepared to handle the customary mechanical problems that can interrupt your cycling enjoyment.

But the book goes farther, providing detailed information on repairing a broken spoke and overhauling a crank.

Amply illustrated with over fifty photographs and line drawings, *Basic Bicycle Repair* will answer many of your questions about frequently occurring maintenance problems.

Many thousands of cyclists have truly discovered that once they have been liberated from worry about possible mechanical breakdowns, the world opens up to their wheels.

James C. McCullagh
Editor/Publisher
Bicycling magazine

Listening to Your Bicycle

Roger Bergman

The visual spectacle of the operating bicycle is very satisfying—but also very distracting—when trying to track down mechanical problems. Bicycle parts, moreover, move very quickly, and you can't watch them while you ride. But you *can* listen and you can also feel vibrations.

As a general rule, for all sounds, normal and abnormal, the cadence of the sound is as important as the quality of the sound. Try to match the tempo and rhythm of the sound to the tempo and rhythm of some rotating part of the bicycle by moving different parts separately.

Cadence Versus Quality

It is perfectly normal to hear a soft, rapid, clicking noise from a rear derailleur hub while coasting. This is the ratchet mechanism within the gear cluster that enables you to coast or freewheel. Pedal forward and the sound should stop while you engage the ratchets (called pawls).

If the chain runs forward by itself while you coast with the pedals stationary, then you have a friction freewheel at the rear hub, and the front freewheel mechanism will click from the bottom bracket.

While coasting, 3-speed bikes will click from the rear hub in all three gears; and while pedaling, a slow clicking in the first and second gears is normal, too.

You may, on the other hand, hear abnormal sounds. If you hear a clickety-clack similar to the freewheel ratchet but louder and with a distinct rhythm, there is probably something wrong. Does the noise quicken as the wheels spin faster and slacken as the wheels decelerate? Do you hear it both while pedaling and coasting? Spin the wheels separately to determine if the sound is from the front wheel or the rear wheel. Look for something striking some or all of the spokes as the wheel spins. Check the end of your kickstand, a stray gear or brake cable, or even the edge of a 3-speed chainguard. A reflector bracket, baby seat, or basket part can also make this clickety-clack, which will persist while pedaling and while coasting as long as the wheel is moving spokes past the noisy item.

A slower ticking accompanied by a muffled vibration, both pedaling and coasting, is rubber striking metal somewhere as the wheel spins. You can usually feel this problem while pushing the bike slowly a few yards. Look for a wheel out of true where a rim catches a brake pad one or more times in every revolution. The tire can also touch a fender or the frame and make a similar sound. Don't overlook inaccessible places such as the reflector bolt sticking through the rear fender on a 3-speed.

The Crank that Clanks

Other noises do not persist while both pedaling and coasting. If the sounds stop while coasting, we can eliminate wheel problems since the wheels are still turning. Remember that we are matching the rhythm of the sound to the rhythm of some moving part of the bike.

A clank that you hear exactly in phase with rotating the cranks implies that something is hitting the crank. These clanks can be caused by the kickstand, chainguard, and also by bent chainrings. You can usually hear these problems while rotating the cranks in either direction, and occasionally you will discover a loose bottom bracket at the same time. When the clank takes on a scraping quality, check the front derailleur cage (chainguide).

Clanks that do not match the rotation of the cranks and that stop when you coast are almost always caused by the chain. In addition, the chain may chink as well as clank. Check the entire chain, including the chainguard if you have one. Remember that the chain usually has enough slack so that gravity will deflect it downward when not under tension. I can usually crouch behind the bike and sight along the chain to examine it. Also, investigate the bottom of the large chainring if you are crosschaining.

A crunching clank heard only while you pedal may be the chain trying to decide between two ambiguous gears. Adjust the gear levers, including wing nuts, if you have them. Other derailleur adjustments may also be necessary.

Straight crunching at any time, or as some people describe it, cracking, is very bad news. Crunching will be accompanied by looseness or by variations in the resistance of the bad part, or both. If heard only while pedaling, examine the bottom bracket, rear hub, and pedals. Otherwise, check the headset and both hubs.

You will find ball bearings ground into hemispheres and cubes, gears without teeth, dented caps, and other masticated parts. Unfortunately, parts that have deteriorated to this point will require replacement. Resolve to lubricate and adjust more often.

Squeaks are the hardest category of noise to track down. Those that you hear all the time, regardless of the motion of the cranks or chain, are usually in the hubs and require lubrication. Once in a while they are benign, such as saddle springs or spokes rubbing together in a tight wheel. Check the headset by turning the handlebars while you lean on them.

An Appreciable Squeak

Squeaks that stop when you coast are one of the following and can be cured with lubrication: bottom bracket, pedals, or rear derailleur pulleys. It is probably easiest to oil the derailleur first before you start taking things apart. But since these squeaks may appear only under pressure, you may wind up greasing all three before you finally find the culprit.

A groan each time you push down hard on the pedals may be from another cyclist trying to keep up with you, but it is probably a pedal asking for lubrication or your cotterless crank coming loose.

People sometimes complain of squealing brakes. Explore the adjustment of the pivot bolts, but do not ever lubricate the rims. Ordinarily, the vibration of the brake pad against the rim when the brakes are applied may be embarrassing, but will not affect the efficiency of the brakes. If the brakes work, I suggest not tampering with them, although there are two cures for the squealing.

One cure is to bend the calipers slightly so that the front part of the brake pad meets the rim before the rear. Since the calipers are designed to be stiff and to resist bending, you risk snapping the calipers. A safer solution may be to remove the pads and shave off a few millimeters at the rear of the brake pad, again so the front of the pad meets the rim first.

Some noises occur only when going over a bump and do not correspond to pedaling, coasting, or anything else. These noises are mostly rattles. Check such features as fenders, chainguard, lights, reflectors, and accessories. Three-speed bikes often have a noisy ornament on the front fender. I usually tap each part of the bike with the fleshy part of a finger until I track down the rattle.

Many rattles are benign, but others can be extremely dangerous: a loose bolt that lets a fender rattle may be the same bolt that secures your brake calipers; a loose kickstand may fall into the spokes; a loose basket may jam your wheel and throw you headlong into traffic.

By and large, noises from your bicycle are warning signals to take action for safety or maintenance. Take them seriously.

Basic Bicycle Tools

Frank Berto

When buying your first bicycle tools,* think of three repair situations: emergency roadside repairs, routine home adjustments and maintenance, and annual overhauls.

Roadside Repair Kit

The most frequent roadside failure is a flat tire. Cycling is more pleasant if a flat tire means a ten-minute delay rather than a crisis. In order of frequency, other roadside problems are: broken spokes, derailleurs going out of adjustment, cable failures, loose bolts, and chain failures. Unlike flat tires, these failures usually won't immobilize you.

A good emergency repair kit for short trips and commuting consists of a Mafac repair kit plus allen wrenches for your bike's allen bolts, a small chain rivet extractor, and a ⅛-inch blade screwdriver. The extra tools will fit into the Mafac pouch. The total cost should be under $10.

You will also need a tire pump and a small patch kit. The patches with the Mafac kit don't include glue, and they don't stick very well. Rema makes a fine small patch kit. Or, you can carry an extra tube of glue.

If your bike doesn't have quick-release wheels, a 6-inch crescent wrench will loosen your wheel nuts with less strain than the Mafac wrench.

The suggested roadside tools don't include a spoke wrench because it isn't very useful. The severely stressed rear spokes on the freewheel side are the ones that usually break. You can't replace a freewheel-side spoke without removing the freewheel, and that's

*Prices cited may vary with geographical location and supplier.

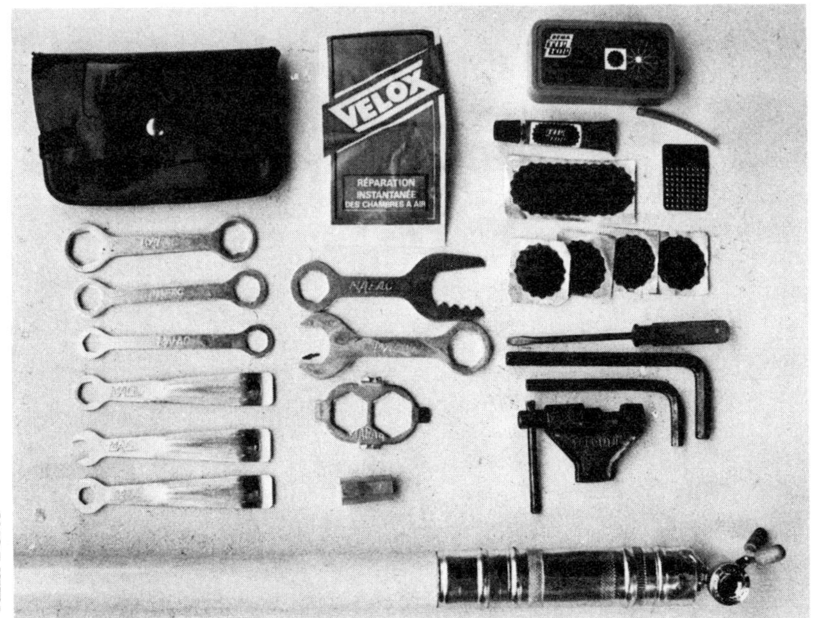

Frank Berto

Photo 1: Roadside repair kit including Mafac and patch kits plus useful tools.

definitely not a roadside job. So, when a spoke breaks, loosen your brake adjustment until the rim doesn't rub and finish out your ride.

Simple Home Maintenance Kit

Your basic home tool kit contains heavy-duty versions of the roadside tools plus a few extras. A good starting kit consists of:

- 6-inch adjustable wrench ($5; Crescent makes a fine one)
- 3/16-inch blade screwdriver ($1.50)
- Pair of side-cutting pliers ($6)
- Chain rivet extractor ($3; if you have a Shimano Uniglide chain, buy their chain breaker)
- Spoke wrench ($3; Park Tool makes a reliable one; be sure to get the size to fit your spokes)
- Brake arm squeezer or third hand ($2)
- Universal bicycle wrench ($1)
- Spray can of WD-40 or something similar ($1)
- Oil can ($1)
- Repair manual (*Richard's Bicycle Book* by Richard

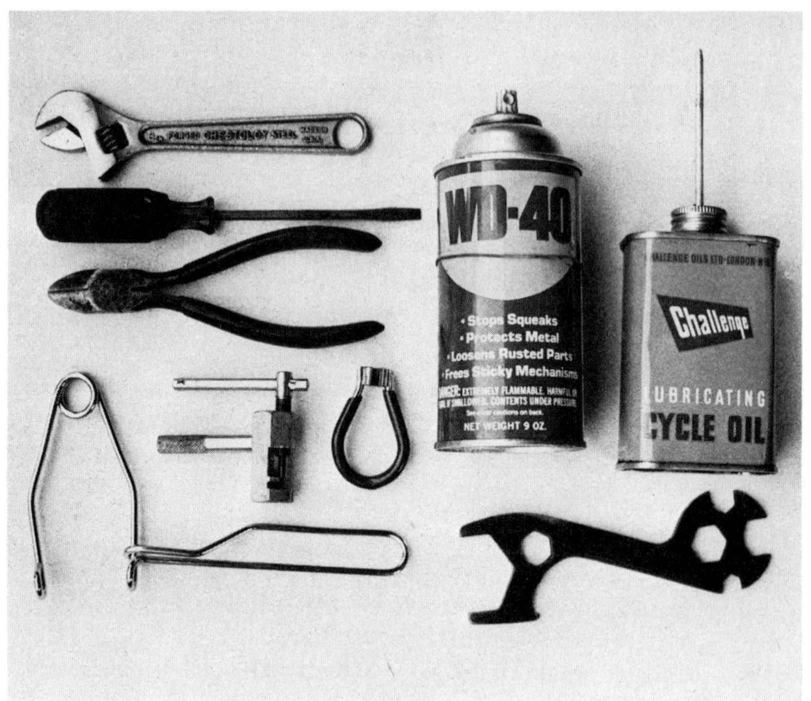

Frank Berto

Photo 2: Simple home maintenance kit.

Ballantine [New York: Ballantine, 1976] is helpful and inexpensive)

With these tools, you can keep your bike clean, lubricated and adjusted, and you can replace tubes, tires, brake pads, cables, and chains as necessary.

The most controversial tool is the spoke wrench. Without a fair knowledge of what you are doing and a wheel truing stand, you'll often do more harm than good.

Advanced Home Maintenance Kit

Most beginners won't need the tools in the following list. However, if you want to do all of your own work, you'll require these tools. Compared to the hourly rates that a good bike shop must charge, the cost of tools is quickly amortized.

For a proper cycle overhaul, you have to have the tools to get

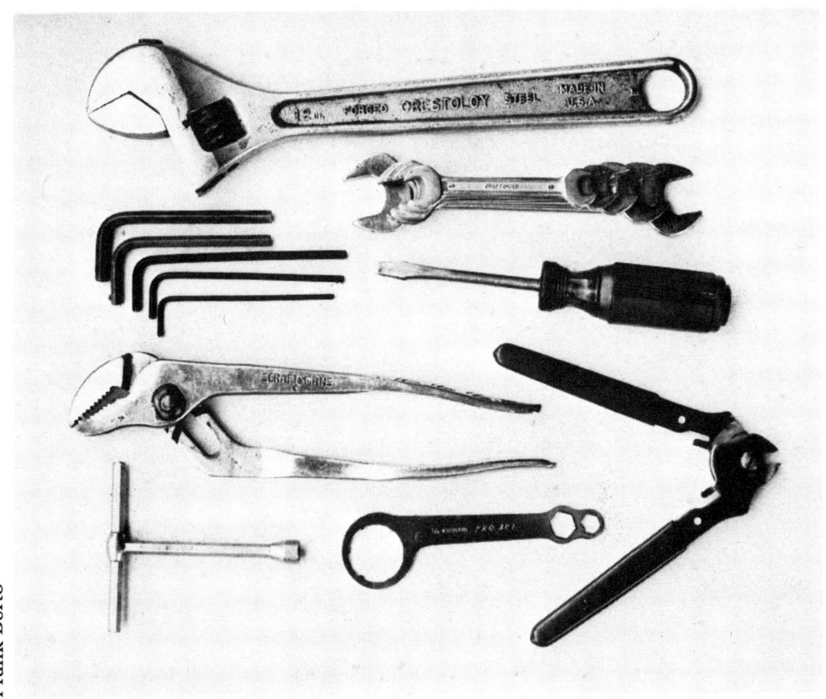

Frank Berto

Photo 3: Additional miscellaneous tools.

into the 14 sets of ball bearings. These tools are like can openers; you need them to get into where the action is.

Bottom bracket tools are needed to change chainwheels and to clean, check, grease, and adjust the bottom bracket bearings:

- Fixed and movable cup wrenches (Campagnolo makes a good set of three tools for $30 that also removes pedals and headsets; Sugino offers two tools for $10; make sure that you get wrenches that fit your bottom bracket)
- Crankset remover ($5; get one that fits your crank)
- Chainring bolt wrench (50¢)

Hub and freewheel tools allow you gear freaks to change sprockets on your freewheel. You can also clean, regrease, and adjust your hubs and clean and reoil your freewheel.

- Cone wrenches ($3/pair; Bicycle Research and Sugino make

quite adequate narrow wrenches; the front and rear hubs are usually different sizes)
- Freewheel remover ($3; get one that fits your freewheel; you will also need a vise or a 12-inch adjustable wrench)
- Chain-type sprocket removers (At $5 each, you need two of these, or one and a special freewheel vise)

Miscellaneous Tools

- Arc joint pliers ($7)
- Metric open-end wrenches ($5; a set of five wrenches measuring 8 to 17 millimeters across the open end works for most bikes; for some strange reason, the 16-millimeter size is left out of most sets, but it's a common bicycle size)
- Metric allen wrenches ($4)
- Pedal dust cap wrench ($2)
- Cable cutter ($9; Sun Tour makes a fine one)
- ¼-inch blade screwdriver ($2)

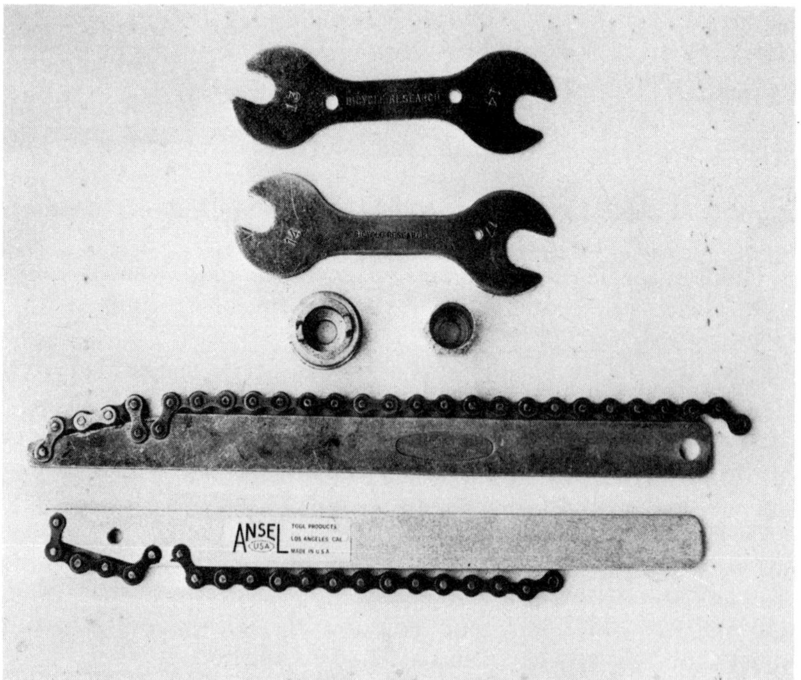

Frank Berto

Photo 4: Hub and freewheel tools.

- Campagnolo T-wrench ($6; high priced but it fits so many parts)

If you get seriously into home bicycle repair, you'll need a comprehensive repair manual. I recommend the following four:

- *Glenn's Complete Bicycle Manual: Selection, Maintenance, Repair,* by Clarence W. Coles and Harold T. Glenn (New York: Crown, 1973)
- *Derailleur 5, 10 & 15-Speed Bicycle Repair,* 2d ed. (Canoga Park, California: XYZYX Information Corporation, 1972)
- *Sutherland's Handbook for Bicycle Mechanics,* 2d ed., by Howard Sutherland (Berkeley, California: Sutherland, 1974)
- *DeLong's Guide to Bicycles & Bicycling: The Art & Science,* by Fred DeLong (Radnor, Pennsylvania: Chilton, 1978)

More Bicycle Tools

Richard Jow

Have you ever wondered about some of those intriguing tools that hang on the tool boards of your local bike shop? You can't figure out what they're used for simply by their looks—but you know they're for *something*.

There are certain tools that are used only for setting up a bike, and some are used when, unfortunately, your bike gets a little bent. I've picked a few of these strange-looking tools in order to explain their uses.

Ever have trouble with your wheel rubbing? If you brought your troubles to the shop, the mechanic would first check the dish or centering of your wheels. For this he'd use a dishing tool.

If the wheels are OK, he'd check to see if the stays or forks were out of alignment. The fork centering gauge does this. This tool has a fixed width to fit exactly between the fork tips or dropouts. Fixed dead center on the part that fits between the tips is a sliding pointer bar. If the forks or stays are not bent, this bar points to the brake mounting hole. If it doesn't, you'll know the forks or stays are bent.

Ever have trouble lining up the tension and jockey wheels of the rear derailleur with the cogs of the freewheel? If you have, you might find that the dropout is bent. Solution: bend it back. There's a proper tool for this operation and it isn't a 12-inch crescent wrench. The alignment tool for this job, actually a pair of tools, is also a gauge. Its purpose is to get the cups to line up with each other. The long T-handles provide a means to tighten the tool on the dropouts, as well as giving the necessary leverage to bend them.

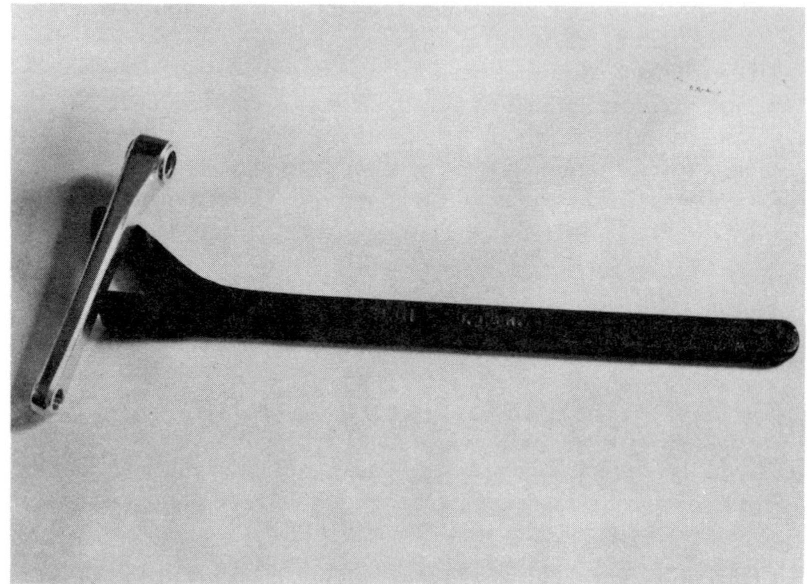

Richard Jow

Photo 5: Crank straightener.

Did you scrape your pedal or spill the bike on one of the pedals? Usually, one crank gets a little bent when this happens. For this there's an unbender. It's a heavy lever which will bend almost any crank without too much strain. When using this tool, remove the crank from the axle first, or the bottom bracket alignment might be affected.

Another crank tool whose use and appearance don't seem to relate is the chainwheel straightener. This is a simple bar of tool steel with an S-slot cut into each end. One of the slots will fit the warped chainring. It's a simple chore to take the wave out.

Bump into something? If you bumped hard, the wheel could have flattened out a bit, or worse, the forks might have had their

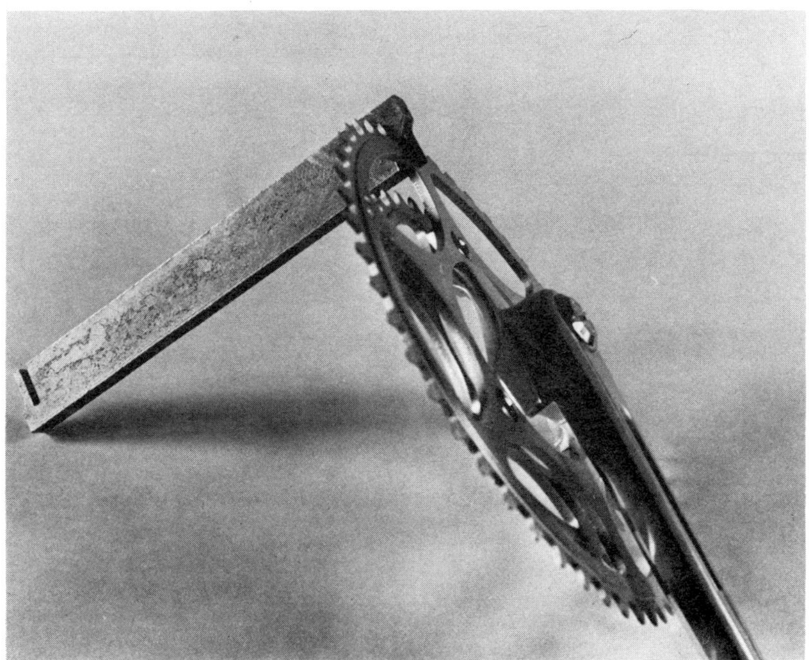
Richard Jow

Photo 6: A chainwheel straightener on a chainwheel.

offset changed all of a sudden. If the damage is not too bad, there are some tools that'll put it all straight (or curved) again.

The strange-looking rim straightener tool is not used very often, but when it can be used, much time is saved because the wheel doesn't have to be unlaced. All the wheel needs, after the concentricity of the rim is restored, is a bit of truing, and you're ready to go. A caution, though: if the rim straightener is used too zealously, you'll end up with a rim that has a bump on it instead of a flat spot.

Speaking of wheels, are you interested in making your own spokes? If you are, there's a hand-operated spoke threader tool available. Its primary use is to clean up threads that may have gotten damaged or to extend the amount of threads on a spoke. This is a great way to save on the spoke inventory a shop would otherwise have to carry. Just get the longest spoke that is expected to be used, thread what you need for shorter lengths, and cut off the excess. Of course, you won't make any money, but just think, only one drawer of spokes.

The spoke threader looks like a miniature lathe and it operates

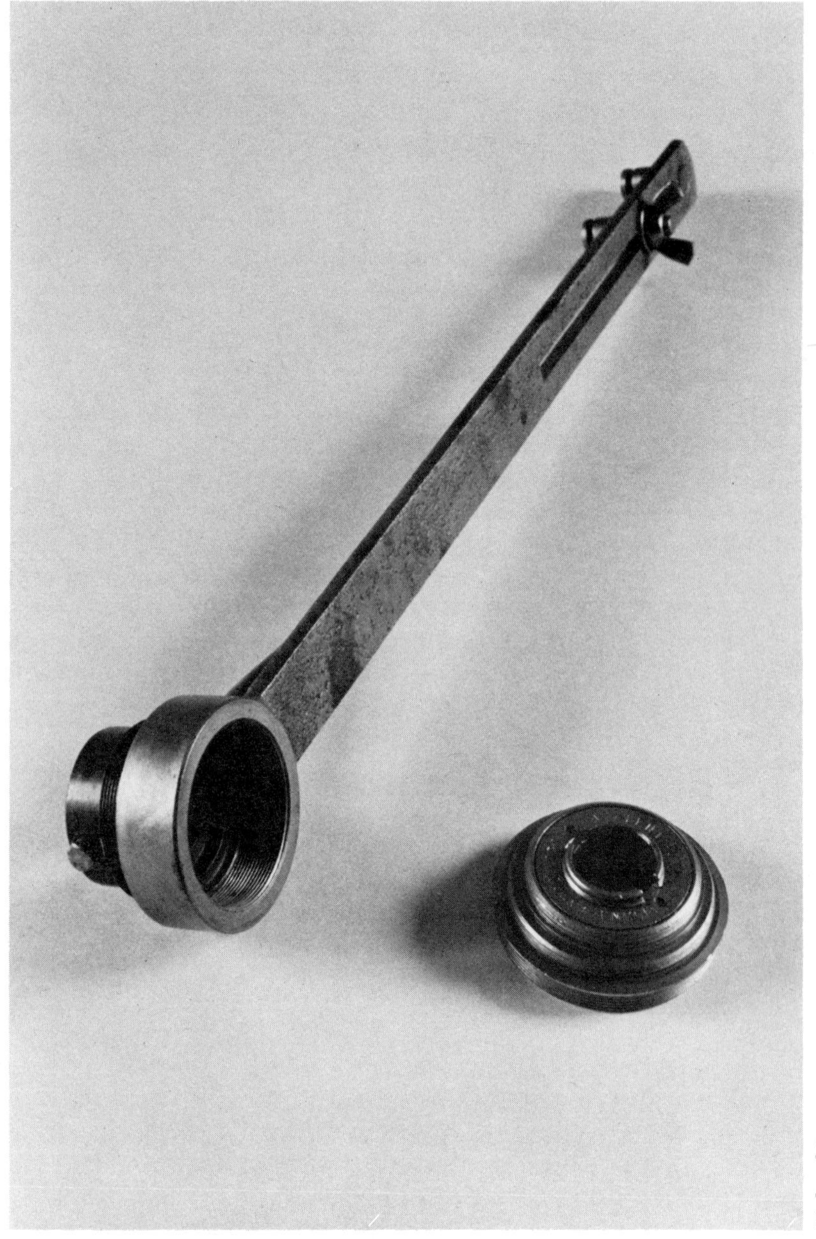

Richard Jow

Photo 7: Regina freewheel body wrench.

in almost the same way. A spoke is clamped into the fixed end. This keeps it aligned, while the movable end with the die and crank handle are engaged onto the spoke. The handle is cranked and the threads cut.

Has your frame suffered severe damage, whereby the forks have changed in geometry? A handy tool for this is the fork vise or clamp. The tool is clamped in a vise, and the forks are clamped within it. The smooth-angled jaws of the fork vise are ideal for circular shapes because they have at least four points of contact to keep the forks from revolving. If you work without this tool, you run the risk of damaging the forks with gouges, flat spots, vise jaw marks, and new curvature because you cannot grip them in the right place.

If you work a great deal on Regina freewheels, a good tool to know about is the freewheel body wrench. It has a long handle with a threaded knob at one end. At the other end are pins which hold the biggest cog on a freewheel while replacing cogs or removing or replacing the cover plate.

The reason for this tool's existence is the way the last two cogs are fitted onto the Regina body. The Regina has all of its cogs threaded to the body. This eliminates the play that eventually develops on freewheel bodies designed on the splined method of mounting the cogs. With the Regina, the last two cogs are threaded on from the back of the body. Because of this, these two cogs must be left-hand threaded. If not, in a short time, chain force would loosen the cogs, and then they'd fall off, leaving you with a 6-speed bike.

After removing the three smaller cogs from the front in the normal manner, simply screw the body into the threaded portion of the knob, making sure there's plenty of thread engagement. Next, screw the handled part of the knob until it bears tightly on the body. This acts just like a locknut immobilizing the body. It's then a simple chore to remove the two larger cogs with a chain wrench.

A Roll for Your Tools

Eugene LeVee

How do you keep your tools handy when you are on the road? Did you ever lose one or leave the one you needed at home? Well, I have a solution for you: a simple, easy, sew-it-yourself project.

This tool roll is made of heavy cloth and has separate pockets for various tools and spare parts. It organizes your tools and prevents them from being misplaced or even worse, not taken along. You can tell at a glance if all your tools are there. It will also keep your tools protected and keep them from clanking and bashing against one another or against the gear in your pack. It is useful for both an extensive cross-country tour and an afternoon's outing.

Materials you will need are: a piece of heavy fabric, like denim, approximately 17 × 18 inches (these are the measurements of the one that I made, however, you can custom make your own); heavy thread; 44 inches of ¼-inch-wide cloth tape (or you can use a strip cut from the fabric).

This is how to make it: First set out all the tools you intend to take along on a ride or tour. Place them parallel to each other an inch apart. Small tools can be placed together, such as chain tool and spoke wrench. Each tool or group will be in a separate pocket. You can make a large pocket for miscellaneous items.

Measure the entire length of all the tools and the height of the longest one (see figure 1a). Add 2 inches to the length, double the height, and add 3 inches (see figure 1b). This is the size fabric you will need. Write down the widths of each tool pocket.

Hem the fabric on all sides. Fold the fabric along its length so the two edges are parallel and 3 inches apart. Stitch each of the tool pockets to the widths you have recorded (see figure 1c).

To make the ties, take the cloth tape or the strip of fabric and fold it in half. Sew the fold securely near one edge in the middle of the end pocket. Your tool roll is complete (see figure 1d).

This is how to use it: Place your tools in the pockets and fold down (see figure 1e) the top edge over the openings of the pockets. Roll (see figure 1f) toward the side with the ties, then wrap the ties around and knot (see figure 1g).

I recommend double-stitching all seams. You may leave more fabric on either side of the pockets—making it longer than necessary—thereby creating a softer roll. I have used this tool roll on many trips, and it has served me well.

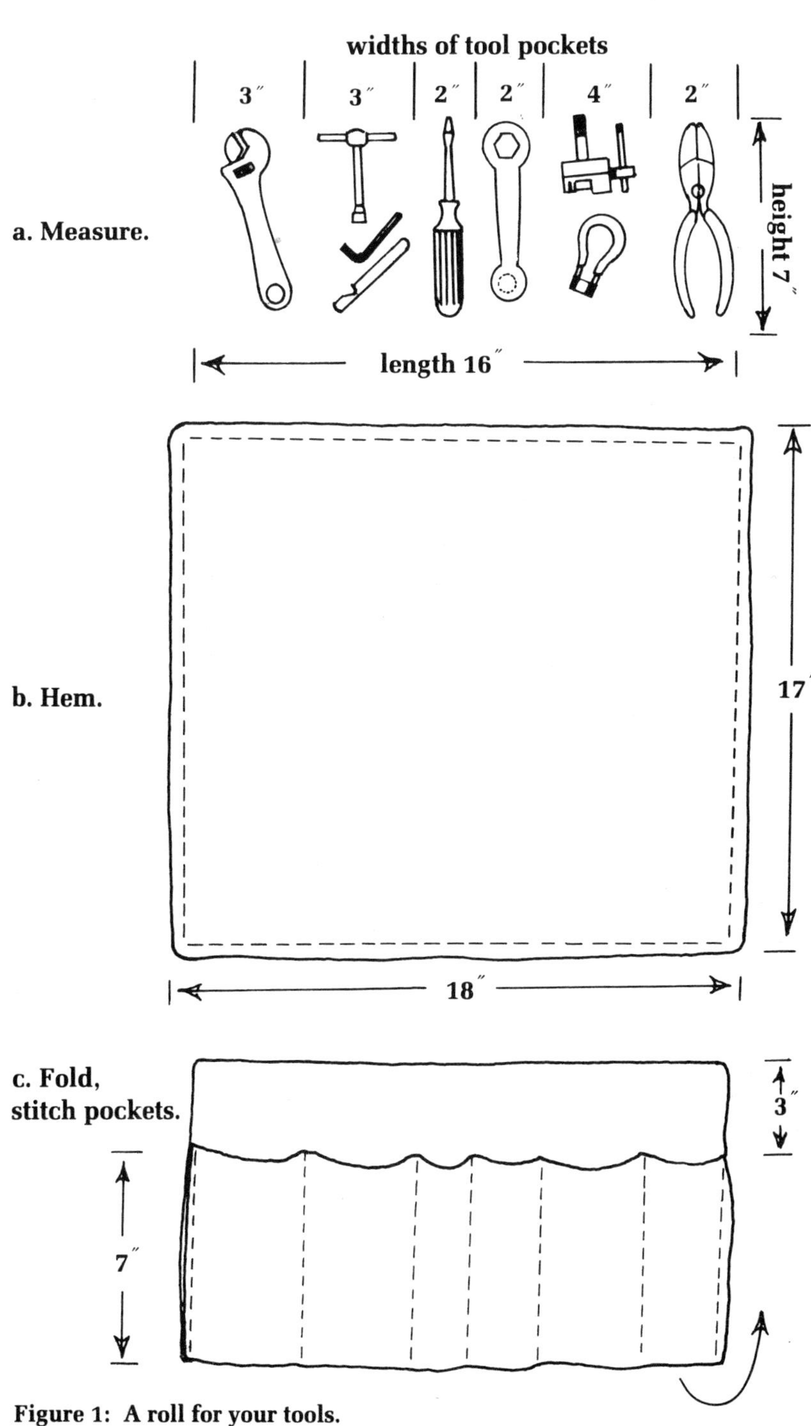

Figure 1: A roll for your tools.
(continued on next page)

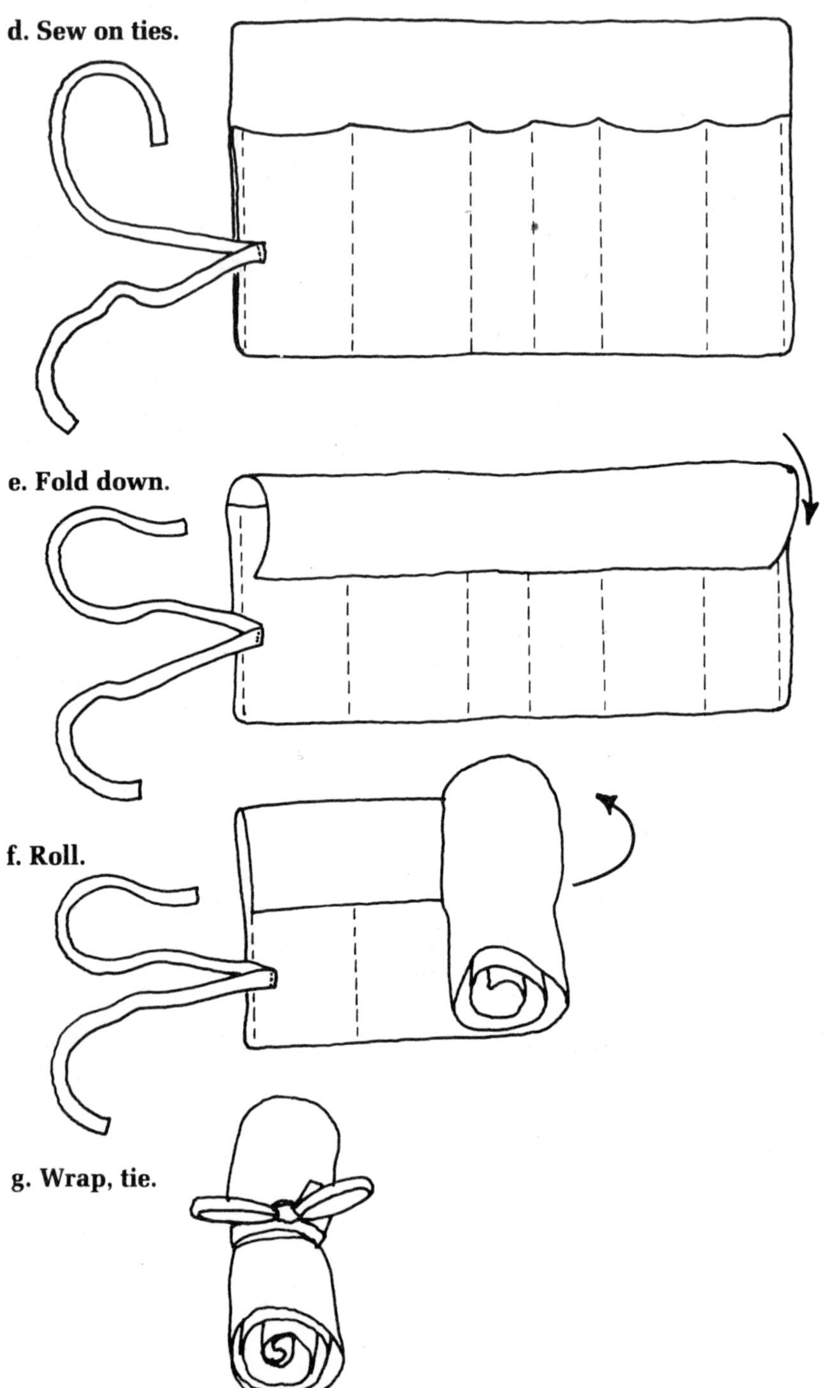
d. Sew on ties.
e. Fold down.
f. Roll.
g. Wrap, tie.

Preliminary Maintenance

Carolyn Gard

One advantage of riding a bicycle is that it runs well on very little maintenance. Riding a bicycle without maintaining it can also be a disadvantage. One consequence of not caring for the bicycle, apart from an accident, is that one neglected problem leads to a problem elsewhere that can't be ignored. Another problem occurs when you have to endure the wrath of the bicycle mechanic as he tells you your bicycle is a machine and not a toy.

It's possible to do preventive maintenance on your bicycle without truing a wheel, taking the hub apart, or replacing the derailleur.

First, take a look at your bicycle to get acquainted with it. Find out what kind of derailleur, frame, pedals, and brakes it has so you can give this information to the mechanic if you take the bike into a shop.

Try to remember what your bicycle looks like when it is in good condition. Is there a wire sticking out of the bottom of the derailleur? Are there dust caps on the ends of the pedals? What other knobs and screws are there? What do the teeth on the freewheel look like when they are in good shape? What does an unworn brake pad look and feel like? Check the spokes to make sure they are all straight. Look at the tires to see that there are no weak spots. Make sure the rim isn't bent.

Once you've learned how your bicycle looks, get to know how it feels when you ride it. The gears should shift smoothly, and the chain should not slip off the teeth. If the gears never work properly, and you can't get the bicycle to stay in gear, there is something wrong. You may need to tighten the screw next to the gearshift control lever, or adjust a screw on the derailleur. If you haven't been oiling the chain, it may have dried out and stretched. That means the purchase of a new chain and, possibly, a new freewheel. You can't always put new chains on old sprockets.

A word of caution—anytime you use oil, remember that a little goes a long way. Too much oil on a part will only collect dirt.

Braking should be smooth and efficient. If there is a bumping feel as you brake, there may be a dent in the rim of the wheel. Such a dent can cause the brakes to grip unevenly, leading to excessive tire wear at one spot. You probably got the dent, or blip, when you hit a pothole. Ideally, you should avoid potholes, but there are times when you have to hit one or be run over. Even though your bicycle still runs with the blip, the wheel is likely to be out of true. Take the wheel off and get the whole thing repaired or replaced before you have a more disastrous accident.

If you can't stop at all when you put on the brakes, the brake pads need replacing. Every time you use the bicycle check the brake pads to make sure they still have rubber on them and feel springy. Since you took the time to look at the pads before they were worn, you'll know when they are past their prime.

If you have to squeeze the brake levers more than 2 inches before you stop, the brake cable is too loose. If there is an adjusting screw, you can do the tightening immediately; if you neglect it, you may eventually need three hands to pull up the entire cable.

Check the tires for wear. There may be no tread left, or small cuts in the tire, both of which can lead to a blowout and an accident. Make sure your tires are not underinflated. An underinflated tube can't take the bumps that an inflated one can; there is not enough of an air cushion between the tire and the metal rim.

The derailleur, which moves the chain from one gear to another, is a fragile part of the bicycle. You abuse it if you drop the bicycle on that side. Since you know what the derailleur looks like in good condition, you'll know if it has been damaged and needs repair; you won't have to wait until you can't shift anymore.

All parts of a bicycle benefit from a maintenance check every now and then, even the pedals. If a pedal is loose, find out how to tighten it before it falls off when you are 5 miles from home. The pedal has a metal piece on the outside called a dust cap. This does just what the name says; it keeps dust and dirt out of the pedal assembly. Occasionally the cap gets loose and falls off. If you hear something fall off as you are riding, go back and find it. Then, since you are familiar with your bicycle, you'll know it's the dust cap for the pedal and you won't decide it was just something in the road that came from someone else's bicycle.

The parts on a bicycle are out in the open, making a bicycle easy to repair, but allowing dirt to get into the mechanism. At least once a week, and every time after a ride down a dusty or muddy road, wipe off your bicycle so the dirt doesn't get a chance to work its way into the insides.

If taking a bicycle apart is not your idea of a way to spend a Saturday, don't feel badly about having a mechanic work on it. Be sure to take it in once a year, preferably during the slow season in January and February, and have it lubricated and tuned up. With a little preventive maintenance on your part during the rest of the year, the mechanic won't have to declare your bicycle a disaster when you do bring it in.

Troubleshooting the Frame and Accessories

Chuck Harris

A crabbing bicycle (see figure 2) with wheels plainly out of line is a familiar sight to a following bicyclist. The rider is probably unaware of his steed's condition, and unconsciously compensates for its tendency to pull toward one side when control is relaxed, but it requires a professional balancing act to ride this machine "no hands."

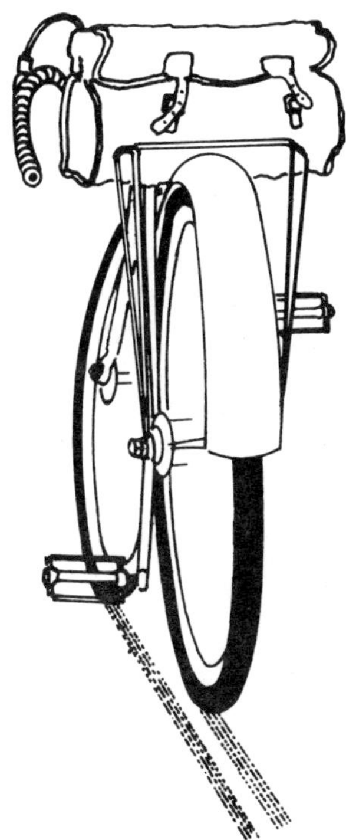

Figure 2: A crabbing bicycle.

This wheel misalignment could result from an improperly dished rear wheel, or more likely, a seriously twisted frame or fork. The latter requires knowledgeable treatment which is beyond the scope of the average home workshop.

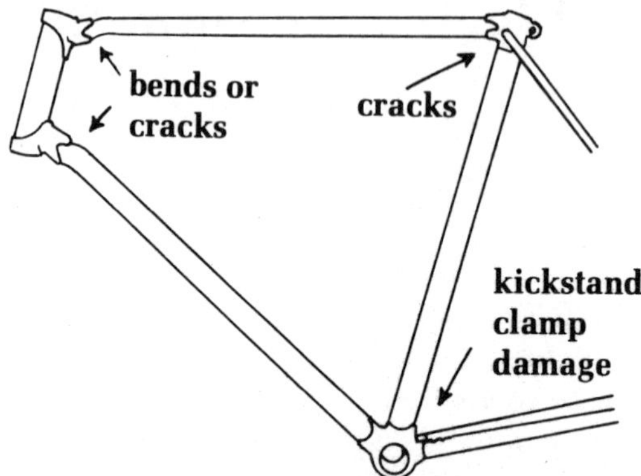

Figure 3: Points to check for common frame damage.

Frames can be damaged in other ways by collision, overload, or can even succumb to faulty design or construction. Figure 3 shows typical collision damage to the head joints. If these bends are restraightened by brute force, it is quite common to find the down tube cracking away from its head lug some miles later. Seatstays can be cracked free of the seat lug by a swaying load on the rear. They can be reinforced and rebrazed by an average mechanic. Sometimes the jaws of a kickstand clamp will mar the chainstays where they leave the bottom bracket. Dents here don't damage the frame seriously, but cracks do.

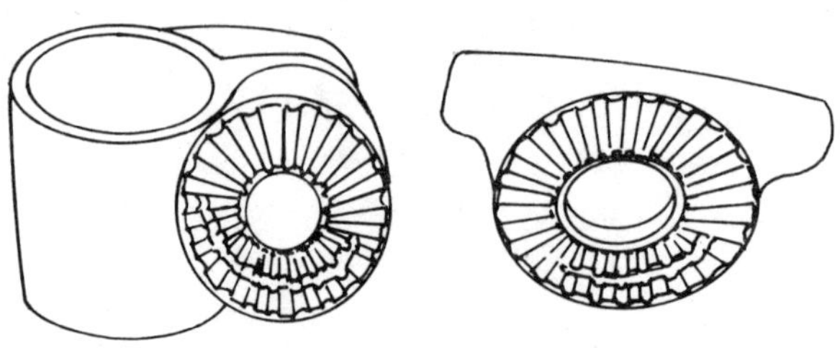

Figure 4: Stripped seat clamp.

The saddle has been clamped to the seatpost by a serrated rotating clamp (see figure 4) for generations. Now some more durable precision screw clamps are available on high-grade equipment, but the average bicycle on the street will be prone to loose, tilting saddles for years to come. If the saddle ever gets jolted to another position (usually quite painfully), it is likely that the serrations are stripped, and will no longer support the rider's weight no matter how much the bolt is tightened. In an emergency, swap left and right plates to mesh with some undamaged teeth, but replace the clamp entirely as soon as practical.

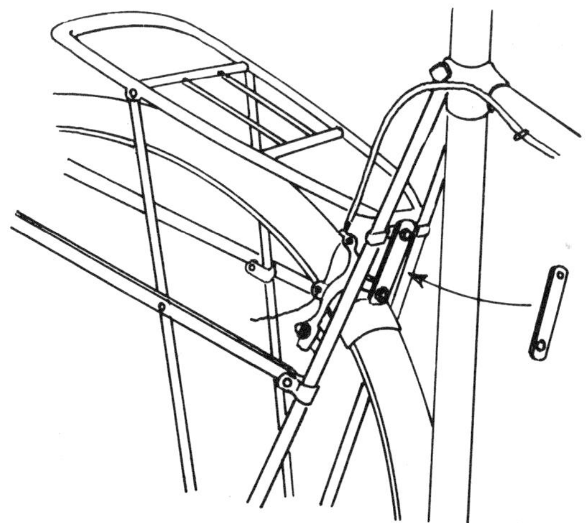

Figure 5: Luggage carrier vertical stop and pannier support.

The luggage carrier, even when thoroughly tightened, poses two possible hazards which should be recognized. One is that the seatstay clamp (if not hung from the seatpost bolt), no matter how tight, might slip downward under load and foul, disable, or lock the rear brake. Some form of vertical stop is necessary. Figure 5 shows one of many possible methods of securing against carrier slip. The second hazard is pannier bags fouling the spokes. Few simple carriers properly support these bags, so the addition of simple lightweight members for this purpose is necessary with their use. Illustrated is a suggestion utilizing aluminum shelf standards (available from hardware stores) and two screw clamps each.

The pump is capable of fully inflating any bicycle tire if it is in

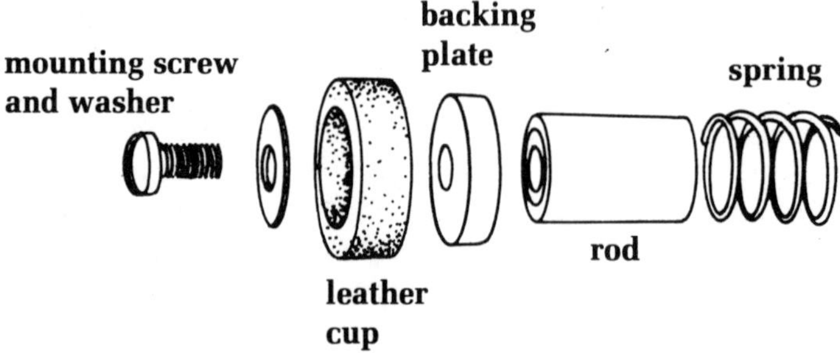

Figure 6: Pump piston assembly.

proper working order, the hose is intact, covered and has soft washers at each end, and the valve doesn't impede airflow. Figure 6 illustrates a typical pump piston. If the pump doesn't hold pressure when stopped by your finger, the leather cup may be dry, cracked or inverted, or the holding screw may be loose. A sick piston cap may be softened with oil and temporarily pressed back into shape, but should be replaced. Missing hose washers may be scissor-cut from plastic bottles. Presto valves are easy pumping but Schrader valves are not. Figure 7 suggests removing the external Schrader valve spring to achieve effortless pumping. Just remember always to use a valve cap afterward! A pump hose connector with a valve depressor is undesirable as it allows too much air to escape while being removed, and frequently its internal check valve restricts airflow.

All types of bicycle electrical equipment are trouble-prone. Battery lamps suffer contact trouble due to corrosion and even improper battery design. (Eveready batteries have a separate plated disk on the negative terminal to retard leakage. It's only held on by a cardboard crimp, and contact to the battery zinc can is assured

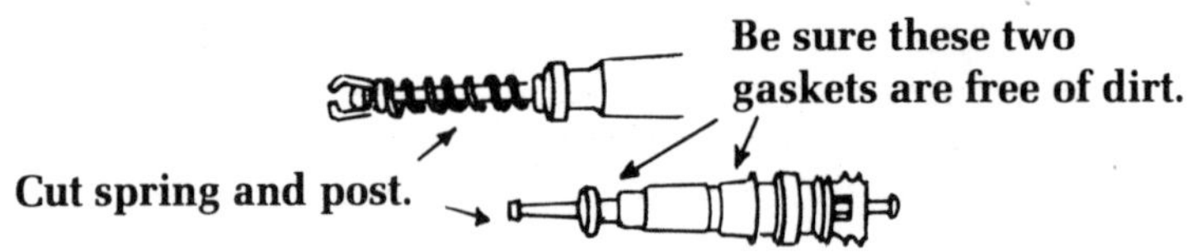

Figure 7: Schrader valve spring removal.

only by strong external spring pressure. Side-by-side battery clamps don't always apply much pressure, and internal corrosion often insulates the battery's negative contact. Fix by peeling this back plate off the battery.) Generator light systems often use only one wire and depend upon the frame and head joint for the second conductor. It is always best to add a second wire from the generator clamp bolt to the casing of headlights and taillights.

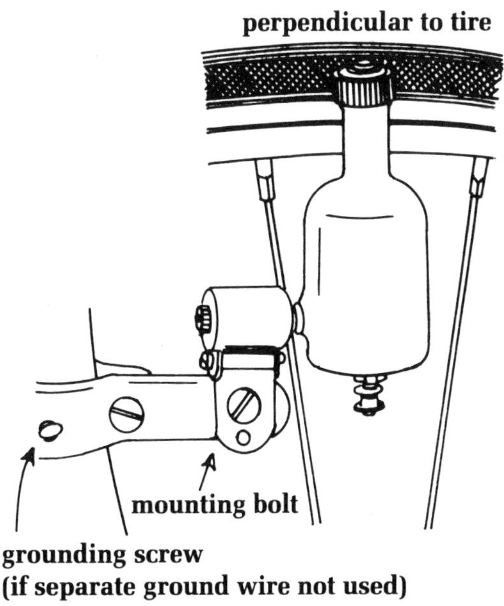

Figure 8: Generator mounting.

The generator clamp bolt (see figure 8) is important and must be secure, with the generator truly radial to the tire at its contact point on the outer sidewall. If considerable resistance is felt (magnetic or frictional) to turning the armature by hand, or if the armature pulley is wearing smooth, the generator will slip on the tire when wet, and should be replaced with a modern multipole free-turning unit. Some aluminum case generators begin to work loose from their mounting boss, and must then be replaced. It is difficult to obtain quality smooth reflectors on modern bicycle headlights. But it is possible to obtain clear replacement 6-volt 0.5 ampere bulbs (G.E. 425 or 605) for the undesirable frosted bulbs now supplied. A small bright spot ahead of the bicyclist is able to illuminate the shoulder against oncoming traffic. A diffused headlight beam is worthless under these conditions.

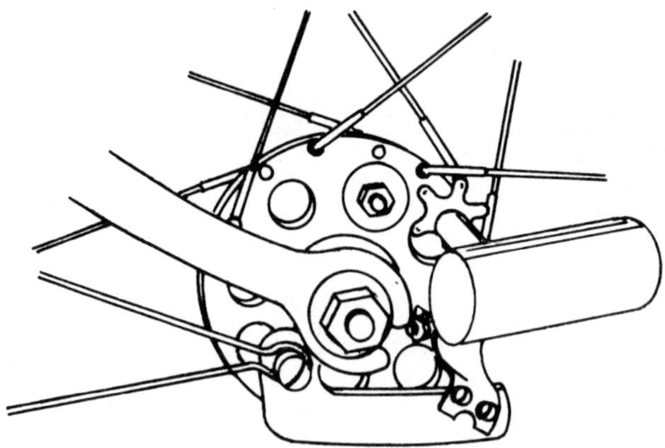

Figure 9: Noiseless cyclometer. Mount the cyclometer close to the hub and use a plastic screw for the striker.

A final troublesome accessory is the cyclometer. They become noisy and often at high speeds the star wheel actually coasts midway between positions and gets hit head-on by the onrushing striker. Figure 9 suggests that you take off the striker and put it in your tool kit for emergency cable repairs. Shorten the cyclometer bracket (the giraffe-necked cyclometer brackets supplied today were inspired by the Raleigh Dynohub) and mount the cyclometer as close to the axle as shown. With high-flange hubs, screw and washers in a flange hole make a quiet striker, particularly if plastic. Low-flange hubs might utilize a two-piece striker or a homemade screw plate at this same radius. The manufacturer's instructions still apply about locating the striker near the star wheel boss.

Troubleshooting Your Gears

John Schubert

Pity the poor derailleur. Whenever a bicycle doesn't shift well, people assume it's the derailleur's fault. The blame is often misplaced. True, the derailleur is the kingpin of the bicycle's intricate shifting mechanisms. But it works in close contact with many other components: the chain, chainwheels, freewheel cogs. Any of these, especially when coated with dirt, can cause poor shifting, scraping, grinding, and other drive train problems. In this chapter, we'll examine the drive train and fix these problems one by one.

It's no fun cleaning greasy dirt out of your drive train, but it's the best way to start an attack on drive train problems. Dirt sneaks into bearing surfaces and other nooks and crannies, so parts which should move freely get gummed up. Cleaning out this dirt will magically cure some problems, and it will make the solutions to others more obvious.

First, the Chain

We'll begin with the chain, partly because it's simple, and partly because a freshly cleaned and oiled chain works noticeably better.

Chains won't last forever, and you should expect to replace yours every couple years, especially if you ride a lot or let the chain get rusty. When the chain wears out, the link pins chew at (and enlarge) the holes in the chain's inner sideplates, and the chain will have too much flex in all directions. Not only does this make for more reluctant shifting (because the chain has a tendency to flex sideways as it spans the gap between the derailleur and the cog), but also each chain link becomes slightly longer. As a result, the chain no longer meshes with the cogs and chainwheel teeth, and grinds them. It also tends to skip up over the teeth of the smallest rear cog when you pedal hard.

To check for chain wear, reach for a section of chain wrapped around a front chainwheel. Using thumb and forefinger, try to pick a single chain link up off the chainwheel teeth. It shouldn't move

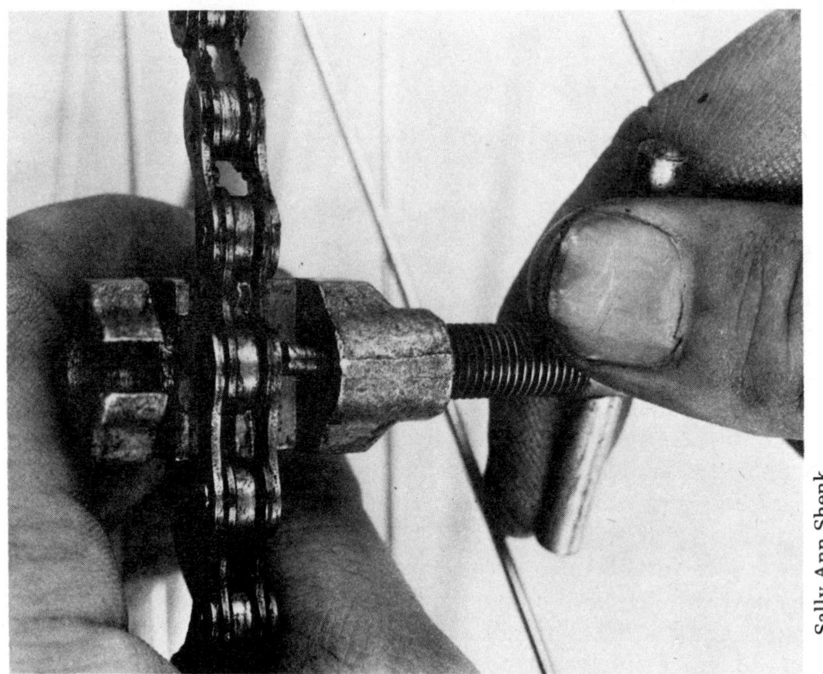

Sally Ann Shenk

Photo 8: When you reassemble a chain, you should restore sideways flexibility to the link you've operated on. Use the chain tool's special notches for this purpose.

more than 1/8 inch. If it can be moved more than that, there is too much flex in the link pins, and it's a sign that the chain should be replaced.

A more elaborate and accurate way of measuring chain wear is to take the chain off the bike as described below and stretch it out on a flat surface. Measure the length of a 24-link section. A new chain will measure 12 inches. When a chain measures more than 12 1/8 inches, the chain is worn out.

If your chain looks dirty, it is—and it should be taken off the bike and cleaned. A 10-speed chain has no master link, so you remove the chain from the bike by cutting it with a chain-link tool. Set the chain in the tool and screw in the chain-tool punch. The punch will push a chain-link pin out of the link. When the pin is almost clear of the chain's inner plates, unscrew the chain-tool

Sally Ann Shenk

Photo 9: You can see plenty of daylight underneath when you pull a badly worn chain away from the chainwheel teeth. A chain in good condition fits the chainwheel more snugly than this.

punch. You should be able to pull the link apart now. To replace the chain later on, you'll use the same chain-tool punch to push the link pin back where it belongs; then you'll put the link in the chain tool's other notch and screw in the punch to flex the link sideways, restoring the link's flexibility.

Soak the chain in a can of kerosene and clean off any dirt with an old paintbrush or rag. Let the chain dry. When you put it back on the bike, give each link a drop of light oil. Allow the oil to penetrate the links and wipe off the outer plates with a rag; oil on the outside surfaces of a chain only attracts more dirt.

Next Target: Freewheel

Now remove the rear wheel from the bicycle so you can have a closer look at your next target—the freewheel. Is it dirty? Clean away the caked dirt with a screwdriver and finish the job with a rag soaked in kerosene. If the freewheel is exceptionally dirty, remove it from the hub with a freewheel remover and soak it in kerosene. Then let it dry thoroughly, so the kerosene has a chance to drain out of the bearings. Whether you soak the freewheel or not, squirt light oil into the gap between the small cog and the freewheel body to lubricate the bearings. Spin the freewheel so the oil is well distributed among those bearings, and use a rag to clean up the excess that leaks back out. (Note: Freewheels last longer than chains, but they do wear out. If your freewheel teeth have rounded corners from the chain grating on them, this may be a cause of drive train problems, such as the chain skipping on the smallest cog.)

Then, the Derailleur

We're finally ready to examine your rear derailleur. Start this task with the rear wheel off the bike, so you can more easily manipulate the derailleur mechanism. The derailleur has two spring-loaded pivots: one takes up chain slack by rotating the chain cage toward the rear of the bike, and the other pulls the chain cage out (except when the cyclist shifts into a lower gear). A few rear derailleurs have a third spring-loaded pivot which pulls the entire derailleur body toward the rear of the bike.

Get your hands dirty and flex the derailleur along these spring-loaded pivots. When you let go, the spring should snap the derailleur back to its original position. If it doesn't, clean the dirt out and lubricate the mechanism with light oil. Whether you clean the derailleur with a rag or use the immersion method depends on the amount of dirt present. Make sure you thoroughly clean and lubricate the two rollers in the chain cage.

And Last: The Cable

Now that you've cleaned your derailleur so that it pivots freely, you're almost finished. The only procedures left are to clean and grease the derailleur cable (if necessary), adjust the range-of-motion limiting screws, and on a few models, adjust the angle at which the derailleur body rests. Overhauling the cable is a simple operation.

With the rear wheel back on the bicycle, shift to your highest and lowest gears, and observe how wide a range of motion the derailleur has. It should reach just far enough in each direction to sit directly underneath the cogs on either end of the freewheel. If the range of motion needs to be altered, turn the high- and low-gear adjusting screws found on all rear derailleurs.

The last step is only necessary for a few rear derailleurs—the resting angle adjustment. This is best left alone, especially if there's no apparent need to change it. But if the chain sometimes skips over the smallest cog, try turning this adjusting screw counter-clockwise, to position the derailleur farther forward and wrap more chain around the cogs. However, don't change the resting angle so much that the jockey roller collides with the largest cog when you shift into low gear.

Cleanliness is 90 percent of all maintenance required to keep your drive train rolling. The cable overhaul described above will make any derailleur, no matter how cheap or expensive, work quite well.

Cleaning Your Gears

John Schubert

Does your front derailleur obey your wishes? Or does it throw the chain nowhere in particular, make awful noises which you can't get rid of, and respond begrudgingly to your tugging at the shift lever? And does the chain have a mind of its own? These problems can all be fixed with a methodical overhaul of the front end of your drive train.

In the previous chapter we used a little loving care, some kerosene, and a lot of old rags to make the rear end of the drive train (freewheel, rear derailleur, and chain) work better. Overhauling the front end of the drive train is a different sort of job for a few reasons.

To begin with, the front shift is inherently a cruder mechanism. The front derailleur can give only a sideways shove to a chain under tension, whereas the rear derailleur cradles and guides the slack side of the chain.

Manufacturers of moderately priced bicycles have traditionally built the front end of the drive train to more casual manufacturing tolerances than the rear end. Oftentimes, they've simply built them wrong. And it's quite possible that you can improve your drive train's front-end performance with some well-planned grinding and bending. Fortunately, newer bikes need much less of this sort of retrofitting than bikes from the early 1970s and before. And cotterless cranksets are exempt from all bending and grinding.

Cleanliness First

Before you do anything drastic, get out your tools, rags, and kerosene and see how much you can improve shifting performance through cleanliness.

Lift the chain off the chainwheels and around the outside of the large chainwheel. Tuck it back around the rear of the chainwheels, and it will dangle from the rear of the front derailleur's chain cage. This allows you to work on the front derailleur as if the chain weren't there.

You want to see how easily the front derailleur pivots through its range of motion. Most modern front derailleurs swing the chain cage upward as they swing it outward. Some older designs use a push-rod mechanism which moves the chain cage sideways.

Whichever kind of front derailleur you have, you want it to operate without signs of stickiness. Grab it and manipulate it through its range of motion. It should move smoothly, and the return spring should snap it back to rest position when you let go. If it doesn't disassemble the mechanism, clean it, grease the bearing surfaces, and reassemble. If the derailleur cable passes through a short casing, grease that portion of the cable. If the cable goes around a steel turnaround fitting, grease the point of contact with the fitting.

Minimal Clearance

See that the derailleur is mounted as low as possible on the frame's seat tube. It should clear the large chainwheel by only a few millimeters. The chain cage's sideplates should be parallel to the chain. If they are not parallel, rotate the derailleur on the seat tube until they are.

If necessary, adjust the range-of-motion limiting screws to

these specifications. When the chain is on the small front chainwheel and largest rear cog (L-1), the derailleur chain cage's inner plate should not scrape the chain. The derailleur should have enough, but just barely enough, range of motion to meet these requirements.

Sally Ann Shenk

Photo 10: If you bend the nose of your front derailleur slightly, you'll get better shifting performance.

Sally Ann Shenk

Photo 11: You can use arc-joint pliers to bend your chainwheels. Bend carefully.

Scrub Down

If you've done all the above and your drive train still misbehaves, scrub down for bicycle surgery. You're about to improve on the manufacturer's efforts.

The first step is to bend the front derailleur chain cage. This is an old trick good bike shops routinely perform on new bicycles. In the past year or so, a few manufacturers have finally begun to make derailleurs with the appropriate bends built in at the factory.

Take your pliers and gently bend the front of the outside plate about 2 millimeters inward. Bend the inside plate the same distance outward. By giving the chain cage a narrower nose in this manner, you improve shifting performance. The narrow nose derails the chain with greater authority than a lateral shove from the sideplate.

If your bike has a cotterless crankset, you should be finished now. Cottered crank people should read on.

Lateral Misplacement

Lateral misplacement increases lateral chain deflection, and that makes the drive train run and shift poorly. For reasons I do not understand, cottered cranks are built with a great deal of play in their design. The collar-receiving flat spot on the crank axle is about ¼ inch wider than the cotter pin. This allows you to move the chainwheels ¼ inch laterally whenever you remove the cotter pin.

Check the lateral placement (more commonly known as chain line alignment) by putting the bike in L-1 gear and standing behind the rear wheel. Close one eye and look down the drive train. The middle cog on the freewheel should line up with the space between the two chainwheels. If it doesn't, you may want to remove the cotter pin, slide the chainwheels sideways and reinstall the cotter pin. If this is a new task for you, read a good repair book before you jump into it. You may damage the crank bearings if you don't follow the proper procedure.

Chainwheels Too Close Together

Now, with your chainwheels in proper chain line alignment, see whether they're too close together (as they were on so many French 10-speeds sold during the bike boom a few years back). Put the bike in L-5 gear (small chainwheel, smallest cog). The chain should not scrape against the inside of the large chainwheel.

If it does, you should bend the large chainwheel slightly

outward. The best way to do this is with a special chainwheel bending tool, but you can find plenty of usable substitutes in your home toolbox.

Among the candidates for ad hoc chainwheel bending tools are the claw end of a carpenter's hammer, a hefty screwdriver, the part of an adjustable hacksaw frame which ordinarily holds the far end of the hacksaw blade, and any other thin piece of metal strong enough to withstand some sideways bending. Slide your piece of metal between the two chainwheels so one end rests near one of the fixing bolts (the bolts which attach the chainwheels to one another). Bend outward. Do the same for each of the fixing bolts.

Another good bending technique is to use arc-joint pliers. Grip the large chainwheel as close to its center as you can and bend from several points around the circumference.

Interference with a Chainguard

If all this bending causes interference problems with one of those pie plate chainguards, I suggest abandoning it. Rubber bands around the pants cuffs cause less trouble.

Now after all this work, do you still have a drive train problem? One common mishap occurs like this: you're riding along in L-1 gear and the chain spontaneously derails to the inside. Or you're riding in H-1 (large chainwheel, largest rear cog) and the same thing happens. Many mechanics try to "fix" the L-1 derailment by adjusting the front derailleur so it constantly pushes the chain toward the chainwheel. That's incorrect. The derailleur should touch the chain only during shifting.

Dull Chainwheel Teeth

These derailments occur because the chainwheel teeth are too blunt, because of lax quality control and ill-placed lumps of chrome-plating. Top-quality chainwheels have sharp teeth with carefully designed and machined profiles. The chain walks up off the top of blunt teeth, but it stays engaged on sharp teeth.

To make your chainwheels shift like good ones, grab a file and hold it against the side of the teeth. Rotate the cranks and gently grind some metal away. You don't need to do much grinding; a minute or two should be plenty. Don't worry about the ill effects of removing the chrome-plating. Oil from your chain will keep the chainwheels from rusting.

Preventing Derailleur Chain Skipping

Chuck Harris

Skipping is one problem bicycles equipped with a fixed gear system or gear hub rarely experience. In one form or another, it is a common derailleur malady, and will be discussed under the

Sally Ann Shenk

Photo 12: Direction of chain travel.

categories of regular skipping, skipping under load, jamming, spilling, and freewheeling.

Regular skipping—that is, skipping not synchronized with wheel rotation but repeated every few seconds—can usually be traced to one or more stiff or damaged chain links. It is most noticeable on the smallest cogs, and with minimum chain tension. The offending chain links may usually be identified by slowly running the chain backward and watching each link as it leaves the derailleur cage. A stiff link tends to keep its offset as it unwinds from the idler. A twisted chain will show up as it tends to bind and make noise when it passes through the cage.

A stiff link is freed by bending the chain sideways at the trouble point. This operation is usually necessary after riveting a

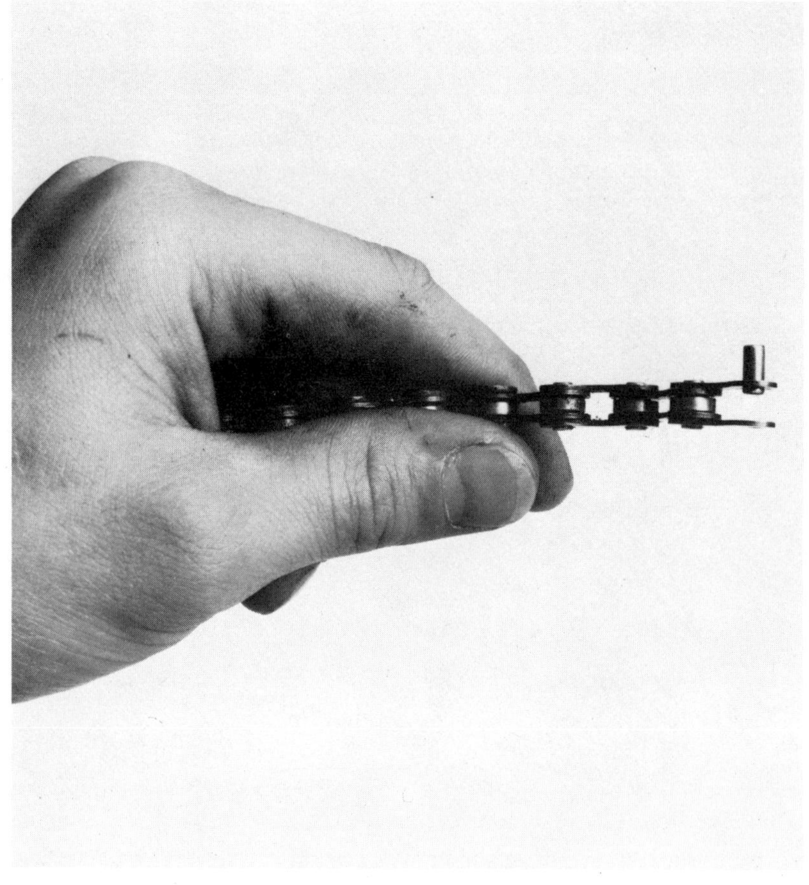

Sally Ann Shenk

Photo 13: Free a stiff link by bending the chain sideways.

chain together. This bending forces the sidebars apart to their normal position. A rusted or otherwise jammed link will require more drastic treatment, or complete chain replacement. It is inadvisable to insert a new link in a used chain because even slight wear actually lengthens the chain (the rivets wear in—a chain doesn't actually stretch). Also ill-advised is replacing a portion of any chain with another make. Rivet sizes, construction quality, and wear resistance vary considerably among chains. A repeatedly noisy section of chain on a repaired bicycle should lead you to suspect a portion of foreign chain.

A twisted chain may be carefully straightened by bending, as long as the sidebars have not been cracked.

Skipping under load is a more serious problem, and frequently results from a mismatch between sprocket and chain. It most commonly shows up when a new chain is used on worn, small cogs (see figure 10). It may also occur with new chain and cogs, but this will usually disappear with use. Cluster cogs are stamped, not machined, and then hardened. At best the resulting tooth finish is quite burred and rough, but no matter how hard, the rough teeth rapidly wear to match the pitch of the chain. For this reason, skipping rarely occurs as the chain wears out, even though the chain pitch lengthens considerably during use. The worn chain wears even the hardest sprocket to match its new pitch, and still performs adequately. The only riding clue to a hopelessly worn chain (see figures 11 and 12) is the sensation of each chain link popping over each tooth under load on the smallest cogs.

Figure 10: Worn cog. Broken line shows original profile. Grind off shaded area to reuse.

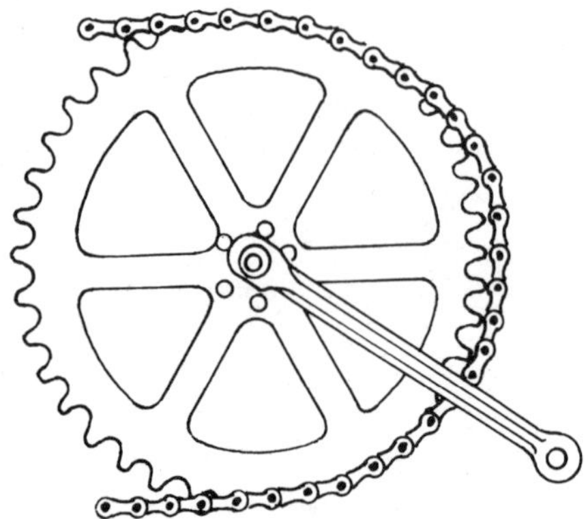

Figure 11: How to identify a worn chain.

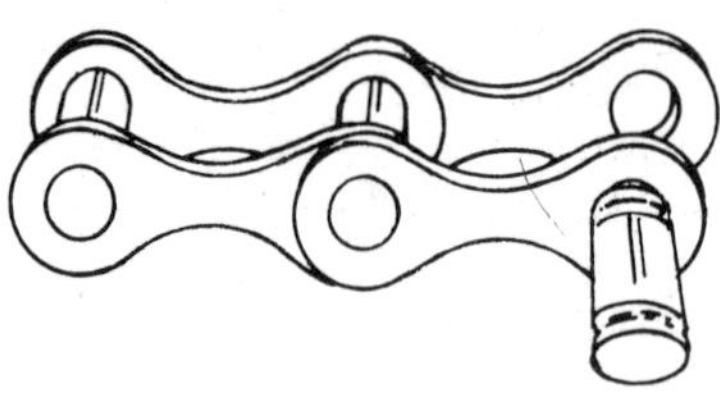

Figure 12: A worn chain will not properly "mesh" with the freewheel cogs, resulting in erratic skipping and inefficient pedaling.

If your freewheel has a worn cog, the teeth won't mesh properly with a new chain. Should you try to use such a chain with a worn cog, a few of the rollers on the chain will bend and, worse, the chain will skip from one cog to another. The skipping will worsen when you're pedaling hard. You can remedy this problem by replacing the worn cog (or the entire freewheel). If you are handy with a high-speed grinder, you might be able to grind the undercut tooth back to a slightly sloping profile.

Sometimes foreign matter such as mud, snow, or grass can cause erratic jumping. The cause in this case is always visible. A much too loose chain (incorrect derailleur chain tension) can sometimes cause load jumping.

Sally Ann Shenk

Photo 14: Chain riveting tool.

Skipping at the chainwheel is rare, and usually results from teeth actually decapitated from wear.

A damaged chainwheel (see figure 13) is about the only cause of wraparound jamming (see figure 14). This problem usually results from the chain shifting between or spilling off chainwheels under full load. It may easily be corrected by filing the damaged teeth back into shape.

Insufficient clearance between freewheel and fork ends may result in jamming when downshifting from high gear (see figure 15). Proper axle spacing is the fix for this unnecessary problem.

Spilling off the chainwheel under load is most commonly a symptom of a warped chainwheel. To correct this, simply bend it

Figure 13: Damaged chainwheel tooth.

Figure 14: Wraparound jamming.

back into line by repeated levering against the bracket by a screwdriver. There is no better substitute for this direct strong arm method.

Spilling does occur quite frequently on 5-speed bicycles, and especially on sidewalk machines. This is a consequence of the chain feeding onto the chainwheel at an angle in all but middle gear. The presence of the front derailleur cage effectively guides the chain into proper mesh, particularly when vibrating sideways. Since 5-speed machines rarely have a two-sided chainwheel guide, their tendency to spill the chain frequently should be weighed against the slight additional cost of the 10-speed machine when buying.

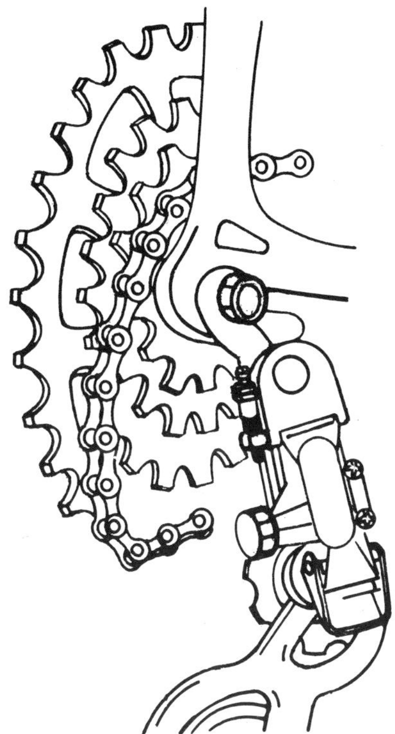

Figure 15: Jamming due to insufficient clearance between freewheel and fork ends.

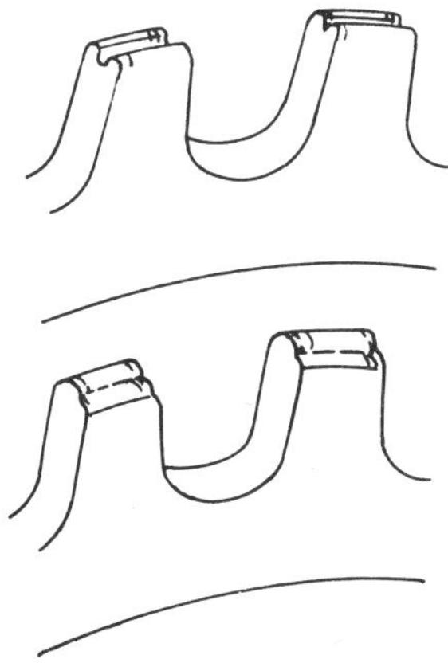

Figure 16: First illustration shows grooves along cog teeth which can cause chain to ride over tooth tips. Second shows either side of the groove may be ground off to prevent chain overriding.

Finally, forward freewheeling is a problem peculiar to deeply grooved, freewheel cog teeth. I will only repeat the observation made in an earlier chapter, that it is frequently possible to shift between gears so that the chain rides in the groove along the tooth tips, resulting in a noisy, complete loss of power. A rapid shift in either direction is necessary to dislodge this hang-up, but the only complete cure is to remove the offending groove from the cog by carefully grinding of one side (see figure 16). In my own experience, this doesn't adversely affect selective downshifting.

Brake Adjustment

John Schubert

It's hard to name a bicycle component more important than brakes. Yet, as any bicycle repairman can attest, most cyclists keep their brakes in minimal repair. How about you? Are your brakes well-adjusted enough to get you out of any jam you might pedal into? If not, an hour of your time and possibly a few dollars can put your brakes in top condition. You probably won't have to redo the job for at least a year.

Possible Problems

Several problems befall brakes. You may find yourself fixing any or all of the following:

Excess friction in the moving parts (hand lever, cable and casing, brake arm pivot points) robs energy from the assigned task of slowing the bicycle down. The friction also fools you into thinking you really are braking hard (because you're squeezing so hard) at a time when you aren't.

Misaligned brake shoes work poorly because the rubber pads don't strike the rim squarely. This can lead to flat tires from sidewall abrasion, rapid and uneven wear of your brake pads, and inferior braking performance. Or your brake pads may be so badly worn, especially if they're worn unevenly, that they need replacement.

If the brake mechanism isn't centered over the wheel, one brake shoe may drag on the rim constantly. While it's possible for this to be a mere annoyance in otherwise well-adjusted brakes, it feels awful. And it introduces a constant drag that obscures the nice

Sally Ann Shenk

Photo 15: When cutting cable casings, use a swift, firm grip and a sharp pair of wire cutters. This will insure a clean cut.

road feel you should get in your fingertips when you apply your brakes.

Your brakes may be too loose, so that you have to squeeze the hand lever almost to the end of its range of motion just to get the brake pads to touch the rim. Too-loose brakes don't give you enough stopping power. Most well-designed brake sets (including some of the very cheapest ones sold) can be adjusted to offer so much stopping power that you'll be squeezing as hard as you can (and locking your wheels) before you run out of lever travel. Your bike should be in such condition.

Brakes may be too tight, so they rub the rim constantly. Or perhaps a warped or dented rim strikes the brake pads as it revolves between them.

Brakes may be mounted loosely on the bicycle frame. This introduces wobble and clatter into the brake system, and also increases the chances of a serious accident from the brake coming off the frame and tangling in the spokes.

Begin your overhaul by making sure your brakes can't come off the frame. Is the nut which holds them onto the frame loose? Or, once you've loosened it, does it spin freely? If it does, it might vibrate right off someday and cause you to crash.

Some brakes have a small rubber ring embedded in the mounting nut. The rubber ring keeps the nut from spinning freely and ensures that the nut won't vibrate off.

If your brakes don't have this rubber insert, invest a dollar in a tiny bottle of any brand of anaerobic adhesive. (Anaerobic adhesive gums up the threads so the nut comes loose only when you want it to.) You may want to put it on other bicycle parts as well, but don't get it near any *moving* parts, and don't use very much. A little goes a long way.

Now look over your rims. They're part of your braking system, and you can't do an overhaul without checking them, too. Lift the bicycle so one wheel is a few inches off the floor and give the wheel a spin. Does it wobble from side to side because of a potato-chip-shaped warp? Use a spoke wrench to fix the warp. Or, if you prefer, have a shop true your wheels for you. But don't neglect this part of the adjustment.

Reducing Friction

The biggest portion of the job will probably be reducing excess friction from the moving parts. Start by loosening the cable inner wire from the brake's binder bolt so you can free the cable from the hand lever.

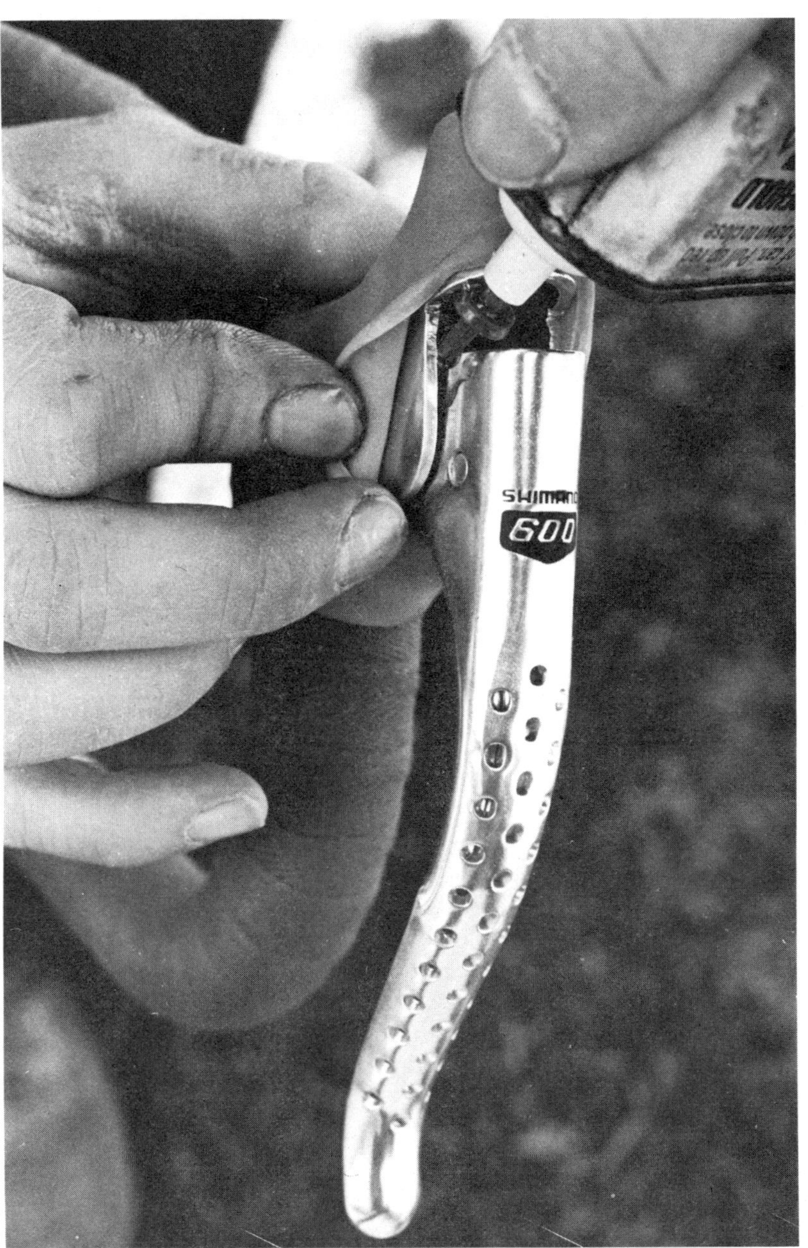

Sally Ann Shenk

Photo 16: A few drops of oil may be all that's necessary to relieve the friction in your hand levers.

Does the hand lever swing freely when the cable isn't attached? If it doesn't, squirt some oil at the hand lever pivot points. Swing the lever several times. If the lever still doesn't swing freely, gently bend it to one side and, while continuing to bend, swing it up and down a few times. Then bend it to the other side and repeat.

While you're working on your hand levers, make sure they're securely attached to the handlebars. If they need tightening, give a firm twist to the mounting screw (usually found in the throat of the lever housing).

Your next target is cable friction, an especially common cause of brake malfunctions. There are two problems here: overall cable casing length, and poor lubrication.

Right Cable Length

Cable casing length is an often ignored but significant source of brake system friction. Your cable casings should be no longer than necessary to reach from the brake lever to their endpoint (either the front brake or the frame's top tube) in a smooth but tight arc. Any extra casing length adds a lot of friction. (If you glance at any photograph of bicycle racers, you'll see they're all outfitted with very short brake cable casings.)

Odds are your bicycle came from the factory with cable casings a few inches too long. To see how much casing length you can do without, remove the inner wire and hold the casing in its normal position on the bicycle. Move the casing to describe a tight arc between its endpoints and cut off the excess with sharp wire cutters (small wire cutters will do the job if they're sharp).

Don't forget the little bit of cable which reaches up off the top tube and down to the rear brake. Bicycles are often sold with this little loop describing a double-S curve. By shortening this little bit of cable, you can eliminate a lot of friction.

Now grease your inner wire. Work as much grease as you possibly can into the space between the inner wire and the casing. It's important that the cable innards stay well greased; otherwise moisture will cause those innards to rust and stick to one another.

Finally, see if your brake arms can pivot freely. If they can't, try lightly loosening their mounting bolt(s). Those bolts should be just loose enough for the brake to function freely—and not loose enough to allow the brake arms to slope sideways. This concludes your friction hunt.

Inspect your brake shoes and rubber pads. If they're worn unevenly, replace them. If they're mounted so they don't contact the rim squarely, loosen the mounting nut and reposition them.

Make sure you tighten the mounting nut securely, but don't overdo it—you can easily snap the nut off. This mounting nut is another good place for a drop of anaerobic adhesive. And if your brakes have been squealing, gently bend them so the front of the brake pads contacts the rim slightly before the rear.

Centering Brakes—the Easy Way

So many people have resigned themselves to having one brake shoe drag on the rim. They shouldn't. Sidepull brakes can be centered in less than a minute once you learn the trick.

For most brands of sidepull brakes, you'll need a special centering tool—an extra-thin, 10-millimeter wrench. If you're lucky, you may find one at your local bike shop (but you may find it easier to devise your own by buying a hardware store, 10-millimeter wrench and taking it to your grinding wheel). You'll also need a regular 10-millimeter wrench.

Put the regular 10-millimeter wrench on the cap nut (also called the acorn adjusting nut) that holds the whole brake assembly onto the pivot bolt. Now put your extra-thin, 10-millimeter wrench on the locknut which sits right behind the cap nut. Tighten the two nuts against one another. Now leave one of the two wrenches on its nut and move the other wrench to the brake mounting nut (also known as tightening the acorn nut) which holds the whole brake on the frame.

Now, by turning both wrenches in unison, you can rotate the brake pivot bolt—and along with it the spring which centers the calipers and brake shoes. With the slightest twist of your wrist, the brake will be perfectly centered over the wheel.

If your bicycle has those new sidepull brakes without a cap nut, the job is even easier. You won't have to hunt for any extra-thin wrenches. The head of the pivot bolt is broached for a 6-millimeter allen wrench. Insert the allen wrench there. Put a 10-millimeter wrench on the mounting nut in the rear, and rotate it.

If your bicycle has centerpull brakes, the job is no more difficult. You may be able to center the brake with your bare hands; see if you can rotate the bridge (the piece of metal in which the caliper pivots and springs are located) by hand. (If you can, that's not necessarily a sign that the brake is dangerously loose, but make sure the mounting nut can't vibrate off.) If you can't budge the bridge by hand, use a large metal-eating tool, preferably a set of arc-joint pliers. Slightly loosen the 10-millimeter mounting nut, use the tool to rotate the bridge, and hold the bridge in position as you retighten the nut.

Sally Ann Shenk

Photo 17: This bicycle came from the factory with cable casings about 5 inches too long. Here you see what the casing should look like when the extra length is eliminated. By shortening the casing, you'll reduce cable friction.

Tightening the Brake Cable

Tightening your cable is another job that drives many home mechanics to distraction. You have to squeeze the brake shoes shut, pull the cable inner wire tight, and tighten the binder bolt all at once. No wonder various companies manufacture a tool called a third hand, and another tool called a fourth hand.

But you and I can do a fine job with just two hands and a little ingenuity. The procedure is the same for both centerpull and sidepull brakes.

To restore your brakes to working order after removing them, first rethread the cable through the loosened binder bolt. Now take a pair of needle-nose pliers and grip the cable just underneath the binder bolt. Rotate the pliers while keeping a tight grip on the cable. You'll wind the cable around your pliers as you would wind spaghetti around a fork. This automatically shuts the brake shoes.

Wind cable until the brakes are as tight as you want them (you want them on the tight side to allow for cable stretch). Now, while keeping the cable wound up, use your other hand (and for most brands, a 9-millimeter wrench) to tighten the anchor bolt. When the

Sally Ann Shenk

Photo 18: A lightweight grease will make your brake cables function much better. Avoid heavyweight axle grease; the difference between heavyweight and lightweight grease is dramatic.

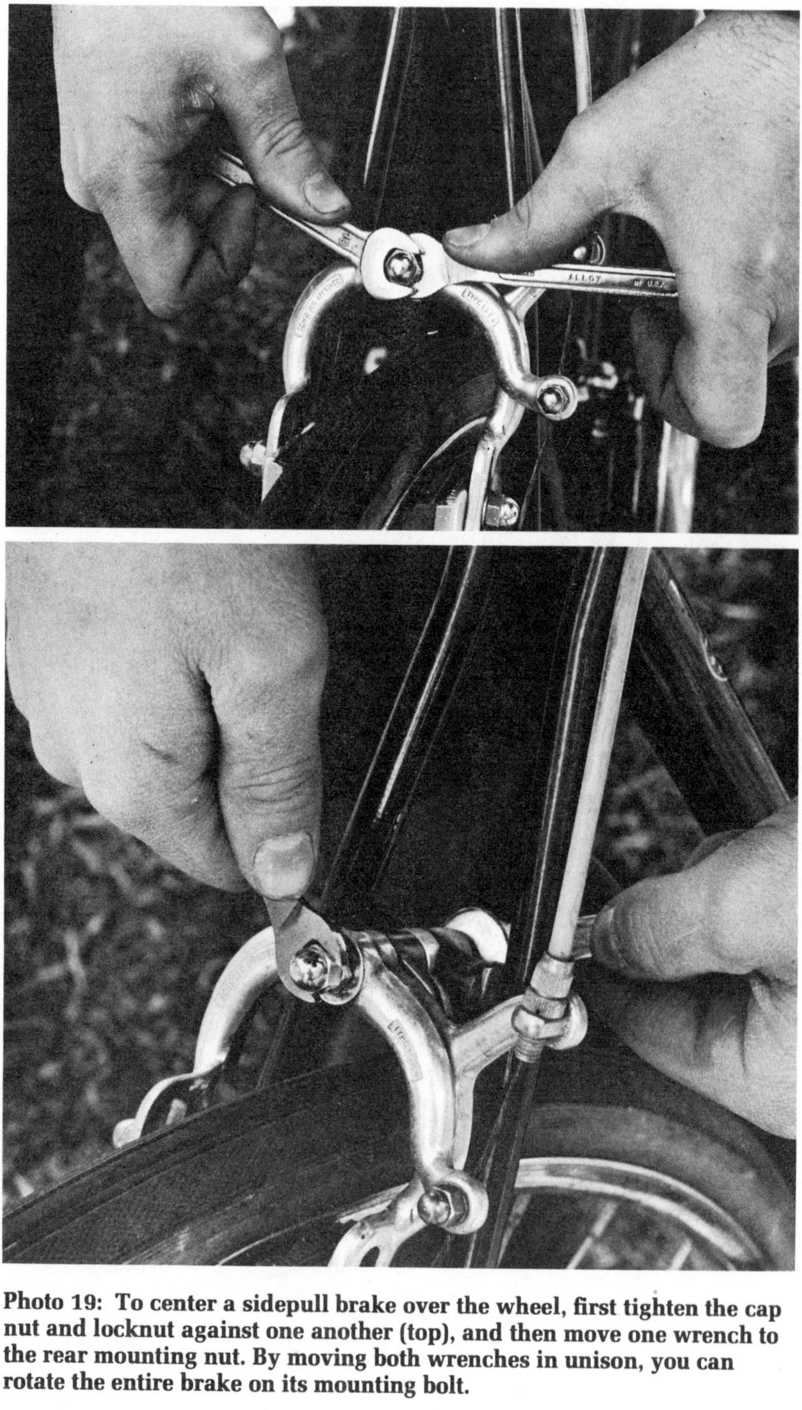

Sally Ann Shenk

Sally Ann Shenk

Photo 19: To center a sidepull brake over the wheel, first tighten the cap nut and locknut against one another (top), and then move one wrench to the rear mounting nut. By moving both wrenches in unison, you can rotate the entire brake on its mounting bolt.

bolt is snug enough to keep the cable from slipping, set your needle-nose pliers down and carefully tighten the cable anchor bolt the rest of the way.

For sidepull brakes, a good rule of thumb is to tighten the anchor bolt as much as you can with one finger. It's easy to strip the threads and snap the bolt off if you use your whole hand. And

Sally Ann Shenk

Photo 20: Two hands do the work of three or four when you attach your brake cable with this method. Grab the cable with needle-nose pliers and wind it tight; use a wrench in your other hand to snug the cable anchor tight.

look at where the cable passes through the hole in the anchor bolt. When it looks substantially crimped, you've tightened it enough to keep it from slipping.

For centerpull brakes, you'll need to finish tightening the anchor bolt with two wrenches, since the anchor bolt is part of that little, free-floating cable yoke. Hold the anchor bolt's rear end steady with one wrench and tighten the nut onto the cable with the other wrench. Your anchor bolt is just as delicate as the one on a sidepull brake, so don't use all your might.

If you have trouble tightening your cable this way, a third-hand tool (available at most bike shops) will hold the brake shoes shut for you. And a household C-clamp makes a very serviceable third-hand tool. Hardly anyone uses the fourth-hand tool.

Now that you've finished your overhaul, be prudent and keep your brakes in good condition. They'll return the favor.

Sally Ann Shenk

Photo 21: For sidepull brakes, the two-handed cable attaching method looks like this. Note that one finger supplies all the strength you need to adequately tighten the anchor bolt.

Basic Bicycle Lubrication

Thom Lieb

Your bicycle components will work more smoothly and last longer if you keep them properly lubricated. If you ride your bike more than once a week, lube once a month; less frequent riders can use a less frequent lubrication schedule.

The best products I have found for lubricating cable are WD-40, LPS-1, and Dri-Slide. These are spray products that come with small extension nozzles for reaching hard-to-get-to spots. All of these products displace water (preventing rust) and do not attract dirt and grit, as do oil and grease.

Spray all the exposed cables and the cables inside the housings, either by using a nozzle or disconnecting and reconnecting the gear and brake cables so you can free the cables. Also spray the cable anchor points on the brake caliper arms (sidepull brakes) or on the cable anchors (centerpull brakes).

Next spray the pivots inside the brake levers, and the shift lever and derailleur pivot points. If you use toe clips and straps, give the strap rollers a shot of lubricant, too.

Some components require more substantial lubricants. You should give each pivot pin in your chain a shot of heavier LPS-3, or a drop of oil, after every week or two of riding. Every month or two, remove the chain and soak it in a can of kerosene. Shake the can to free grit. Take the chain from the can and shake it briskly away from you outdoors. Then soak and shake the chain in clean kerosene, pull out and shake again. Let the chain air-dry, hanging up away from dirt, or dry it with a low-torch flame. Then either soak the chain in a can of warm oil or lay it out with open end up on sheets of newspaper and squirt a drop of LPS-3 oil into each pivot pin. In either case, wipe the sides of the chain with a clean rag to remove excess lubricant—you need lubricate only the pivots. Lubricants on the outside of the chain only attract grit, which will probably cause worse wear.

Use the Right Oil

If you want to use oil, make sure you buy oil designed for bikes, such as Schwinn's oil. Other oils, like 3-in-1, are vegetable-based and will gum up everything. A can of oil with a small spout

Sally Ann Shenk

Photo 22: Spray the derailleur pivot points with a lubricating product to prevent rust.

is easy to use, but a hypodermic dispenser is even handier.

If you ride in the rain, you will have to use a special postride procedure if you want to keep your chain working well. After you come in from a wet ride, apply a penetrating oil, such as Liquid Wrench, to the chain while you turn the cranks and shift gears. This will let the penetrating oil creep in between the pins, rollers, and sideplates, forcing out moisture. Wipe off any excess oil and grime, then apply light oil in the same manner. When the oil is well worked in, allow the bike to set for a few hours, then wipe off the surplus.

After every week or two of riding, you should also lubricate the chain rollers in your rear derailleur. Most chain rollers revolve on metal sleeves and need only an occasional squirt of LPS-3. Some, however, use a ball and cone setup and must be cleaned and regreased occasionally.

Oiling the Hub

If you have a 3-speed bike, you will also have to oil the rear hub occasionally. Locate the oil cap on the hub and flip it open. Add about a tablespoon of oil each month you ride.

Many of the better hubs on 5- and 10-speed hubs also have oil caps, but these hubs always come from the factory with grease instead of oil. To clean or lubricate these hubs, as well as the bearings in your pedals, bottom bracket, and headset, you will have to disassemble the units. All four components work on the same principle: an axle rests between two sets of bearings which are held in place by cones and lockwashers. These cones and bearings must be adjusted so there is no side-to-side play but so the axle spins freely. Adjusting these units requires special tools and a feel that comes only with experience. Unless you know a patient expert who is willing to guide you through the procedure on your first few tries, you should leave this to your bike shop. These components should be overhauled every 6 to 12 months, depending on how often you ride.

The freewheel on 5-, 10-, 12- and 15-speed bikes is the only other component that will need periodic lubrication. You need not lubricate the teeth, but the bearings inside the unit will need an occasional drop or two of oil. This can be added through the gap between the small cog and the freewheel inner body.

Every six months, you should also give your freewheel a thorough cleaning. You will have to remove it from your bike to do so. To remove the freewheel, you will need a special tool made to fit your freewheel. The tool will cost $2-$5. It goes into the slots in

Sally Ann Shenk

Photo 23: Add a tablespoon of oil to the rear hub of a 3-speed bike each month.

the freewheel body after you remove the axle nuts and washers from the rear wheel (if you have quick-release hubs, remove the conical nut and springs). You then screw on the nut (or conical nut) as tight as you can with your fingers to hold the tool in position. On some freewheels, you will first have to remove the inner nut and spacer on the right rear axle.

Use a large wrench counterclockwise to break the freewheel loose. This will take effort. You may have to stand the wheel up and kick the wrench with your heel for leverage. After it breaks free, spin the freewheel off with the tool.

If you want to be adventuresome, you can disassemble the freewheel and clean it. Reassembly can be frustrating, however, so you may opt for a simpler procedure. Here, you clean the cogs of the freewheel with a paintbrush dipped in solvent. Dry them, then flush out the inside by spraying WD-40 into the gap between the small cog and the inner body. Set the freewheel flat on newspaper to let it drain. After a few hours, drop several drops of oil into the body and let it drain again. Then remount the freewheel.

Before remounting the freewheel, squeeze a few drops of oil into the threads of the rear hub. This will prevent the freewheel from sticking. It is also a good idea to lightly grease your seatpost when you insert it or change its position in the frame.

Sally Ann Shenk

Photo 24: Drop a bit of oil between the small cog and the inner body of the freewheel to lubricate the bearings.

Repairing Wired-On Tires

Raymond J. Adams

Bicycle maintenance can be divided into two categories. There is the maintenance you should get done at the shop and the maintenance you should learn to do at home. Tire maintenance and repair are two of the things you should learn to do yourself.

The first thing you have to do is to decide whether you want to use wired-on tires or tubular tires.

Wired-on tires have certain advantages. They are usually cheaper than tubular tires, even when you include the price of the tube. Since they use a lower air pressure than tubulars, they are easier to pump up. Being heavier and thicker, they will have fewer punctures. Under normal wear and tear, they will last longer. They are much easier to repair.

They also have disadvantages. Adding or subtracting weight to the wheels makes it harder or easier to pedal, even on level ground. Wired-on tires are heavier than tubular tires, and the wheels used for wired-on tires are usually heavier. Each tire requires a different kind of rim, so wired-on and tubular tires are not interchangeable on the same wheel.

Wired-on tires are less responsive than tubular tires and require more effort to pedal. Tubular tires are a must for precise, high-speed riding. Wired-on tires are best, however, if you merely plan to ride around the neighborhood, ride on glass- and debris-strewn city streets, or take long rides by yourself where you are all alone, way out in the countryside.

Tire pressures on wired-ons run from about 65 to 100 pounds of air per square inch. Try and get tires with the higher pressures. High-pressure tires give a harder ride and require less effort to pedal, due to less rolling resistance.

When purchasing a tire, check the sidewall. The proper pressure is usually printed there (only on wired-ons). If it is not, be sure to ask the salesman. When purchasing tubes, ask for one made of butyl. All bicycle tires leak because of the high pressure. Butyl tubes are supposed to leak the least.

You will need some accessories. These include a set of tire irons, a patch kit for wired-on tires, an emergency air pump, a regular air pump, and perhaps an air gauge.

Tire irons come in sets of two or three. You can install or remove a tire with just one iron. But try this at home first to make sure you can do it successfully.

The patch kit contains cement, patches, and a grater. Always make sure you have three or four patches, just in case you have a really unlucky day.

The emergency pump is the thin, tubular pump that goes on your bicycle. When buying one, don't forget to get the clips that hold it on to the frame. Ask for a pump for wired-on tires. Do not get a pump that is ultralight. Such a pump saves weight but breaks easily. Remember that this is an emergency pump meant to get you moving again. It's not meant to get your tires up to full pressure.

The two final things you need are a regular air pump and an air gauge. I strongly recommend that you get a pump with a pressure gauge already installed on it. It is a lot easier to use and less time-consuming. You can see the tire pressure as you pump. Get a good, large, strong pump. Those little ones will work you to death trying to get the pressure up.

If you buy a separate air gauge, get it at a bicycle shop. Car gauges do not go high enough, and truck gauges only measure every 5 or 10 pounds.

Proper tire pressure should be measured and not guessed at. However, squeeze the tires every time you pump them up to full pressure. At first, this won't tell you anything. After some experience, however, you will be amazed at how well you can judge tire pressure by this method. Every time I pass my bicycle in the garage, I squeeze the tires. I do the same thing every time I take a break while on a ride. If there has been any significant loss in air pressure, you can spot it right away. When pumping up tires on the road, using the squeeze test is an acceptable way to monitor tire pressure. However, use a gauge when at home. If you are planning a ride, check the tires the night before. Many flats don't occur all at once but appear as slow leaks. Better to find out ahead of time. And if a tire is leaking, don't pump it up and hope for the best. Punctures never get any better.

Always keep a good extra tube on hand at home. If you are planning to meet someone for a ride and you come up with a flat, you can just change tubes and save precious minutes. Fix the punctured tube later.

When you do have a flat, there is a regular procedure to follow. Your first step is to take the tool kit off the saddle. Then turn your bicycle upside down. This way you can open the kit without everything falling out. Go over the tire carefully to see if you can

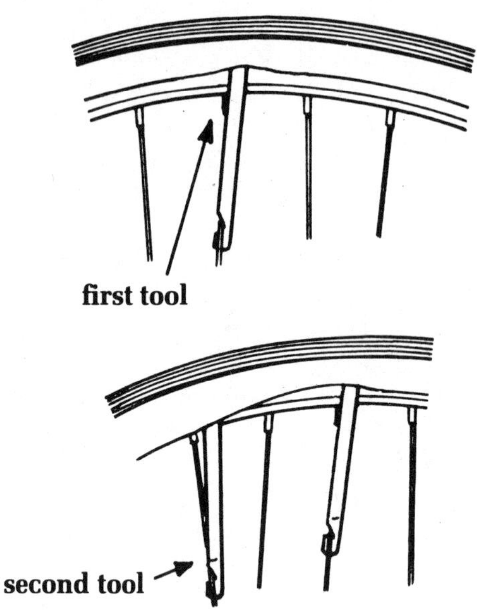

Figure 17: Levering a tire off the rim.

find what caused the puncture. That makes it easier to locate the hole in the tube when you remove it. Check the whole tire while you are at it. You may find something else stuck in the tire.

Remove the wheel from your bicycle and get out the tire irons. Always stop for a moment before removing or installing a tire and remind yourself that tire irons and wheel rims are hard and inner tubes are very soft. Work carefully and don't pinch the tire.

When removing a tire (see figure 17), always start on the side of the wheel opposite the valve stem. When installing one, insert the valve stem first and work away from it.

Take the tire completely off the rim. If you have already located the puncture, put the tire aside and get out the patch kit.

If you haven't found the puncture, start off at the valve stem and go around the tube a couple of times. If you still can't find it, pump up the tire a bit.

If the leak is so bad that you cannot get ahead of it, go back to a visual inspection. The hole is probably large enough to see.

If the tube retains some pressure, look for the puncture. If you still can't find it, hold the tube near one ear and slowly rotate the tube. I have found many a puncture by the hissing sound and the pressure of the escaping air against my cheek.

If you are at home, finding a leak is easy. Just pump up the tube a bit and immerse it in water until you can see the air bubbles. Check the valve to make sure it isn't leaking.

Take a piece of chalk and mark off the spot where the puncture is. Mark it in such a way that you know exactly where the puncture is, even if you can't see it. You can lose the location in either of the next two steps.

Get the small grater out of the patch kit and clean and brush the puncture area. (This is where very small punctures sometimes seem to disappear.) Then smear the area with cement. (This is another time when the puncture can vanish.) Always cover an area slightly larger than the size of the patch you plan to use. Otherwise, the edges of the patch don't stick and you still have a leak. Wait until the cement becomes tacky. Peel the protective cover off the patch and stick it on the cemented area. Wipe off the cement not covered by the patch.

Remember that the tube is curved and the patch is not. If you are not careful, it will come loose at the edges. One way to avoid this is to install the tube in the tire at once and pump it up. If you don't want to do that, then lay the tube on the ground, patch up, and place something over the patch to hold the area flat while you do something else.

Give the tire a thorough examination inside and out. Never quit looking just because you found the cause of the flat. Look for very small objects that have to work their way into the tire to cause a flat. I have found thorns so small I had to spot them with a magnifying glass and remove them with a jeweler's tweezers.

It is an excellent idea to check the tires regularly in any case. Look for cuts, bruises, and breaks that could cause future trouble.

Before reinstalling the tube and tire, check the patch to make sure it is on securely. Get one edge of the tire back on the wheel rim before installing the tube. Start off at the valve stem. You will notice there is a thin rubber strip wrapped around the wheel. This strip protects the tube from the spoke nipples of spoke ends. It has a hole in it where the valve stem slips through. Don't try to jam the stem through the hole in the strip, which is usually made of cheap rubber and breaks easily. Lift the strip, push the stem through, and then put the stem through the hole in the rim. It is a good idea to keep a spare strip at home.

Get the tube around the rim and under the tire. You don't need any tools for this, so just use your hands. Now is the time to be really cautious, because you have to get the second lip of the tire over the wheel rim. This is the time you are most likely to pinch the tube with the tire irons. Be very careful while working the tire back over the rim.

Pump up the tire to 20 or 30 pounds of pressure. Check the stem to see if it looks straight. Then deflate the tire. This may help to loosen creases or pinched spots in the tube.

Your next step depends on whether or not you have quick-release brakes. A quick-release on the brakes is a small device that lets you move the brake pads so you can slip a fully inflated tire between them. If you don't have this quick-release device on the brakes, reinstall the wheel before inflating the tire. Be sure to close the quick-release or the brakes won't work.

Why Flat Tires?

With eight bicycles in the family fleet, I repair a flat tire every other week. I've concluded that flat tires are the result of a variety of causes.

Sloppy riding technique: Learn to steer around glass, pebbles, and potholes. Learn to jump your wheels when you can't avoid a bump.

Tender tires: Tubular tires or the new high pressure, 27 × 1⅛-inch lightweight, clincher tires get more flats. By contrast, the 28 × 1½-inch tires on the Raleigh Tourist I tested are virtually puncture-proof. Unfortunately, easy-rolling tires are more puncture-prone. Wearing out the last 10 percent of the tires' tread will lead to extra punctures.

Weak rims: If you find two rips in your tube, ⅜ inch apart and no sign of anything penetrating your tire, you probably suffered an impact puncture. You ran over a pothole or a stone, and the rim sprang apart, letting the tube bulge out under the tire bead. Low-priced aluminum rims are more prone to this kind of failure.

Excess load: You get many more flats on heavily loaded, rear tires. Heavy riders get more flats than lightweights.

Improper inflation: Riding on underinflated tires leads to more impact punctures. Hammering 110 pounds of air per square inch into tires that call for only 90 also increases the chance of punctures.

You have to strike a balance between punctures on the one hand and responsive, easy-rolling tires on the other hand. The 27 × 1¼-inch Schwinn Le Tour is both rugged and easy rolling. It also is quite expensive.

Frank Berto

Using the emergency pump while on the road can be pretty tiring, especially at the end of a long ride. You might try the system I use. I pump 25 times and rest, 25 times and rest. I do this until the tire is up to a ridable pressure.

Outside of careful riding, there is one way to reduce the number of flats. No tube is puncture-proof, but there are heavier ones that are puncture-resistant. After five flats in one week, I bought a pair. They looked and felt heavy enough to use without the tire.

I found out that I had a new problem when I installed them. I had always ridden with regular tubes. The heavier puncture-resistant tubes made my bicycle seem slower and sluggish. I kept them on for two long rides over one weekend and then I took them off. So if you plan to use such tubes for anything except touring, buy them when you first start to ride. If they are the only tubes you use, they will seem natural to you.

Rotate the tires at least once. It is the rear tire that wears the most and gets the most flats. Exchanging tires will equalize wear and tear. If one tire or tube is in better shape than the other, use it on the rear wheel.

Unless there is a breakthrough in bicycle tire design, there is no way to avoid flats. Careful riding and regular preventive maintenance can keep the number you get to a minimum.

Tubular Tire Repair

Raymond J. Adams

When fixing a flat on a wired-on tire, it is helpful but not necessary to locate the puncture before you take the tire and the tube apart. On tubular or sew-up tires, this is essential. You cannot even begin to fix a flat on a tubular tire until you locate the puncture.

Since the lips of a tubular tire are sewn together, you have to cut through the stitching to get to the tube. By locating the puncture before you start, you only have to cut a few inches of the thread to get directly at the damaged part of the tube. This is why it is important to look for and locate the cause of a tubular puncture as soon as it occurs. The object that caused the flat is still probably stuck in the tire.

If you have already located the puncture, the most frustrating

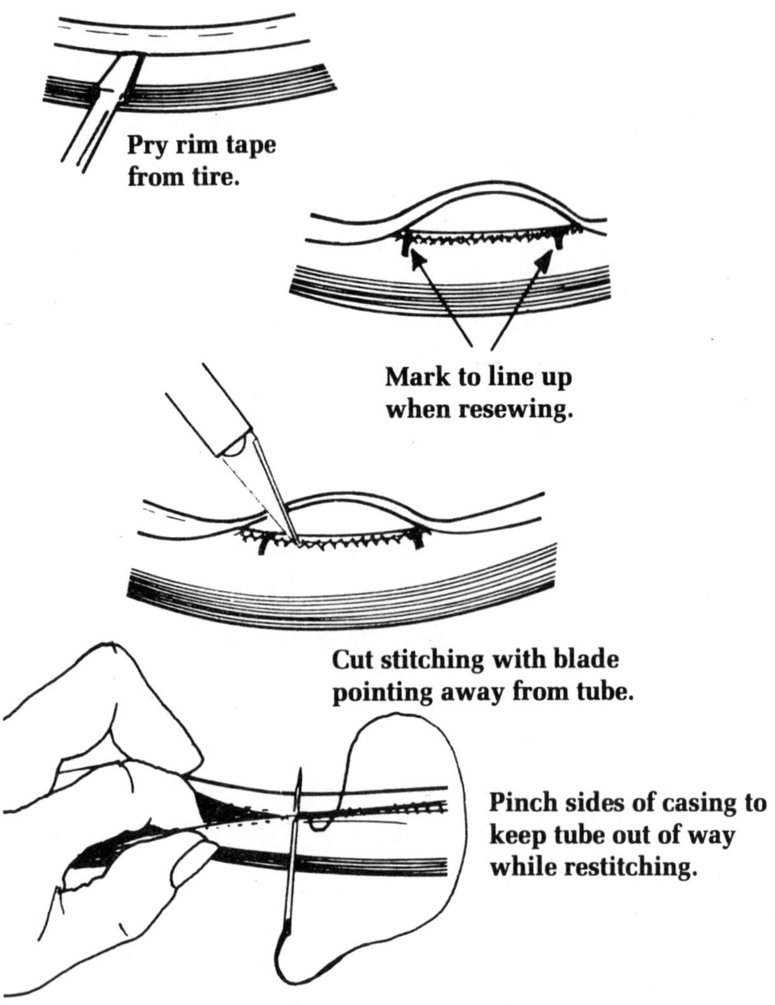

Figure 18: Tubular tire repair.

part of the job is over. If you haven't, your first task is to find it. There are two ways to start. If you have a wheel available, you can mount the tire on the wheel and pump it up to 60 or 70 pounds of pressure. If you don't have a wheel available, you will just have to pump it up as it is.

Start submerging the tire in water, a foot or so at a time, until you locate the puncture. Check the valve to make sure it isn't leaking. Some bubbles may appear near the valve stem. This could possibly mean a damaged stem. More likely, it is just air from the leak escaping out of the biggest available opening. Mark the puncture location once you have found it and deflate the tire and dry it off.

It is now time for surgery. You may know where the puncture is now, but you have as many as three layers of material to go through to get at it.

The first layer is the rim strip. This is a cloth strip glued to the tire. Good fingernails come in handy here. Start picking at one side of the point of the puncture until you work some of it loose. Get a better grip as you go. Right about now your fingertips start to hurt, and you get the urge to use a pair of pliers. Resist it. If the pliers cannot get a good grip, they will tear the strip to shreds. So use only your hands if you can.

If you cannot get the strip loose all the way across the tire, get at least half or three-quarters of the width loose before using pliers. Try to use a pair with wide, smooth tips. Do not angle the pliers as you pull or you may shear the strip. Go gently. Tearing the strip is not a catastrophe, since it can be glued back in place later, but it saves you trouble if it comes off whole.

Pull this rim strip up about 5 or 6 inches on both sides of the puncture. You are now face to face with the stiched part of the tire. Here the two lips of the tube are sewn tightly together.

Use a pair of scissors or a sharp knife to cut the stitches a couple of inches in each direction from the puncture. Since I am clumsy at this, I prefer a sharp X-acto-type knife. Grip the sides of the tire between thumb and forefinger of the left hand and turn the sewn lips to one side. Squeeze the tube so the threads stick out. Slip the blade under a thread and pull out *sideways to your right.* If you cut down, you will cut the tube sooner or later. If you pull upward toward your face, the knife may slip, and you can put an eye out.

Next comes layer number three, a protective cloth between the threaded lips and the tube. For once, you have run into something that is not sewn on or glued down. All you have to do is move it aside and pull out 6 to 8 inches of the tube. If all your guesses were right, you now have the puncture in hand.

If you can't find it, inflate the tire a bit and wet the area and look for bubbles. Mark the spot and dry off the tire.

Before using your patch kit, make sure it is a kit for tubular or sew-up tires and not for wired-ons. The basic tubular kit has two items that are different. Instead of a small metal grater to clean around the puncture, you have an emery cloth. Tubular tires are so thin that a grater would tear them up. The patches are also different. They are much thinner than those used on wired-on tubes.

Smear cement around the puncture. Cover an area slightly larger than the size of the patch you plan to use. When the cement becomes tacky, put the patch on, centering it carefully over the puncture. Make sure it is on securely.

Once this is done, it is time to do what a surgeon does. And that is close up and get out. Put the tube back in the tire and cover it with the protective cloth. Sprinkling the tube lightly with talcum powder helps it slide back into place.

Your tubular tire patch kit has three items lacking in clincher tire kits. These are a needle, thread, and a thimble.

The thimbles are usually made of plastic. It is a good idea to throw them away and get a metal one. I cracked one and only luck kept me from driving the blunt end of the needle an inch or two into the tip of my finger.

When sewing up the lips of the tube, don't start at the break. Start where there are still good threads. Slip the beginning end of the thread under the first few stitches. Use the thread doubled. And use only the thread that comes with the kit.

After you have taken one look at the stitching done at the factory, it is obvious that you cannot duplicate it. You do not have to. Follow a pattern much like a coiled spring going over and under, over and under.

Make sure the holes are aligned when you start so they do not get out of step. Some cyclists make marks across the lips of the tire before they cut the threads. Before sewing it together, they line up the marks. Be careful not to sew the tube to the tire. Finding out after you have gotten the tire together again that you still have a flat is not one of the high points in a cyclist's life.

Leave the last loops slightly loose. Slip the needle and thread under them and tighten them up, but not too tightly or you will cut the tire. Cut off the extra thread.

Use rubber cement to glue the rim back on the tire over the threads. Make sure it is on straight. Give it a few minutes to dry.

You should be building up layers of new cement on the bicycle wheel while working on the tire. If the cement isn't ready yet, check out the rest of your bicycle while you wait. If you are using tape, simply put it on the wheel and go ahead.

When installing the tire, always begin at the valve. Be sure it is fully and comfortably installed before going on. Slowly work the tire onto the wheel. Check carefully to make sure it is on straight. Work it back and forth until it is.

The cement holding the tire to the wheel should be given several hours to dry before using your bicycle. So pump the tire up to pressure and let it stand, preferably overnight. Cyclists who use tubular tires recommend that the tire pressure be reduced when the bicycle is not in use. This is one time to ignore this rule and let the pressure hold the tire firmly on the wheel until the cement sets.

This sounds like an involved and nerve-racking ordeal. And it is until you get the hang of it. I once cut open nearly 3 feet of a tire before I found the puncture. I had no intention of sewing all that up, of course, but after hunting for the puncture for an hour, I was determined I was going to find it. After I found it, I threw the whole mess away.

After doing several tires, it becomes a lot easier. Learning to fix a tubular tire should be looked upon as just another skill to be learned, similar to shifting or braking.

Patching Your Tire and Tube the Cheap Way

Dwight Filley

If you are tired of paying 15¢ for a patch every time you puncture, recent advances in chemistry have given you an alternative. There are several brands of shoe repair compound now available in sporting goods and shoe stores, among them, brands called Shoe Goo and Shoe Patch. Sold in what look like very fat toothpaste tubes, these are clear fluids with the consistency of thick honey, to be used to build up the worn places on the bottoms of tennis shoes. Whether or not it works in this application I can't say, but it sure works on bike tires and tubes.

To fix a small tread or cord cut on a bike tire (either tubular or wired-on), roughen the surrounding tread area with sandpaper, wipe with a strong solvent such as carbon tetrachloride or lacquer thinner, and apply the compound from the tube. Form a smooth, low mound about the size of a dime over the outside of the cut. This is easy since the compound flows just enough to create an even blob if the surface is held level.

To repair a larger cord cut, use the compound to glue a piece of tire casing or heavy cloth to the inside of the cut. Then seal the outside as described above. The compound is very adhesive, and will adhere to the tread surface as long as the tire lasts.

To patch an inner tube, be sure all the air is removed from the tube, thoroughly roughen the rubber around the puncture with sandpaper, and flow on the compound as was done on the tire cut.

In either case, keep the blob level for 15 to 30 minutes until it sets enough not to flow, and don't use the tire or tube until maximum strength is reached (approximately overnight). This is the only disadvantage. If you need that inner tube right now, you better use an old-fashioned patch.

I have patched scores of inner tubes using this method and have had only one failure. In that instance, I left a little pressure in the tube, which slowly blew a bubble in the blob when I wasn't looking. I cut off the solidified bubble and tried to use the tube, but the compound under the bubble was too thin, and I got another leak. Be sure the tube has all the air squeezed out before patching.

As with any glue, adhesion is ruined by grease, dirt, fingerprints, and moisture. Be sure the roughed-up area is clean before applying the compound.

I find this method cheaper and easier than using patches, and for those worried about performance, it is probably lighter as well.

Repairing a Broken Spoke

Ray Wolf

Out of the blue on a midsummer day came the unmistakable sound from my rear wheel: a broken spoke. Not discouraged, I decided, after I had cut the broken spoke off, to keep pedaling. This was my first mistake. Within minutes, three other spokes had failed me—and so did the bicycle shop. The mechanic told me I'd have to wait four weeks for repair. Not content to sit, I tried, with the help of Mike Malekoff, to do the job myself. Here are some of the things I learned from Mike, who has spent many hours building wheels for bicycles on which he raced.

The First Step

The first step in repairing a broken spoke is to remove the wheel from the bike and take it with you to buy replacement spokes. Also, get yourself a spoke wrench and a freewheel remover. They are handy to have.

Then remove the tire and tube from the wheel and clean off any excess grease. If it is a rear wheel and the broken spoke is on the cluster side, you must remove the gear cluster and chainguard. This requires a freewheel remover. With the cluster and guard removed, you are ready to replace the spoke.

By looking at the hub, you can quickly see which way to put in your new spoke. For those who haven't seen spokes close-up before, they are threaded on one end and bent like a fishhook (with a flange instead of a point) on the other end. The flanged end goes into the hub, and the threaded end goes into the rim. A threaded nipple goes through the rim and screws onto the spoke, fastening the spoke to the rim. By adjusting tension on the different spokes, you can pull a wheel into perfect trueness and roundness. (By adjusting the wrong spokes you can make a round wheel square in no time!) To put in a spoke, slip the threaded end through the hole in the hub and pull the spoke into the wheel until the flange meets the hub. At this time, the spoke will not be at its final destination at

Sally Ann Shenk

Photo 25: With the spoke inserted and its pattern traced, begin threading it over and under the other spokes until you reach the hole in the rim. It's all right to bend it; you'll be straightening it later.

the hole in the rim, but don't worry. You still have to weave the new spoke through the old ones to get it where it goes.

Be careful that you have your spoke woven correctly over and under the other spokes. Spokes alternate in their direction from the hub, going in opposite ways. From the hole in the hub where you are going to replace the spoke, skip one spoke and trace the pattern of the next spoke; it will go the way you want the replacement to go. On a three-cross wheel, a wheel where each spoke crosses three other spokes on its way to the rim, the first two spokes are usually crossed on the same side, and the third spoke is crossed on the opposite side.

When moving the spoke it's all right to slightly bend it, as you'll straighten it when tightening. Once the threaded end is through the hole in the rim, recheck its weaving and thread the nipple on until it is snug. Once the nipple is snug, use your spoke wrench to tighten it to about the same tension as the other spokes. The easy part of the job is now over; get ready for the tough part.

Truing the Wheel

Place the wheel in the truing stand and adjust the calipers until they lightly touch the outermost part of the rim when the wheel turns. From this point on, remember that in all operations with your spokes you must do everything in pairs. When truing a wheel you have to realize that if you tighten a spoke that started at the left hub, you have to loosen one next to it that started from the right hub. This will keep the wheel "in round." It doesn't matter what side of the spoke you start with as long as you loosen an opposite one. You should never take more than a half-turn with the spoke wrench at a time: take a half-turn on each pair of spokes in the trouble area and give the wheel a spin to check it before taking another half-turn.

If the wheel is touching the right side of the truing stand (all directions are from a head-on view), you will want to tighten spokes that originate on the left side of the hub. Normally it will take four spokes to pull a minor variation into line. That means you will tighten two spokes and loosen two spokes. If any part of the wheel does not touch the caliper set to within 1/10 inch of the wheel, consider it true.

Now you must check to be sure your wheel is round. Move the calipers up higher onto the wheel until the outer two edges of the rim almost touch the bottom of the caliper arm of the truing stand. Spin the wheel slowly to see if any parts of the wheel touch the stand before others. If any parts touch, tighten the spokes in that

Sally Ann Shenk

Photo 26: The wheel in the truing stand, ready for both truing and rounding.

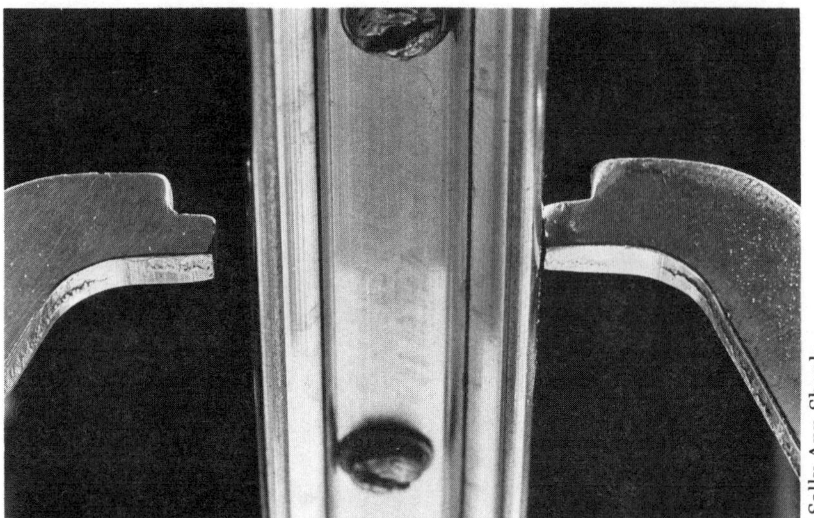

Sally Ann Shenk

Photo 27: The detail shows the wheel to be slightly out of true. The caliper does not touch the left side, so spokes originating on the left side of the hub in that area should be tightened, and those originating on the right side should be loosened.

area to pull that part of the rim up. Remember to always tighten pairs of spokes, one that originates on the right of the hub and one that originates on the left of the hub. This will prevent you from pulling the wheel out of true while you round it. If one part of the rim is too high, loosen a pair of spokes. Once you have it in round, go back and check the trueness, and make necessary adjustments.

When track racers build a wheel, they alternate from checking roundness to trueness until they have no more than a hair's difference in any dimension. For street riding, get as close as you can. Take the wheel off the stand and put it on the floor and apply your body weight to it about every 10 inches around the circumference of the wheel to "spring" the wheel. This will give you a good idea of how the wheel will ride after a few miles. Now, put it back on the stand and check for trueness and roundness. If both are satisfactory, reassemble the wheel and ride on. If not, continue to adjust.

If you are only replacing one spoke, or the wheel isn't too far out of balance, you won't need a truing stand (which can cost $50-$125). If you are making an emergency repair on the road, you can always put the wheel on the bike and use the brake calipers as a truing guide. By alternately squeezing the new spoke and an old one with your hand, you should be able to get a feel for how much tension to put on it. After such immediate maintenance, stop at the next bike shop you pass and have them adjust your wheel.

If you are thinking about doing any long-distance riding, you should practice changing a spoke or two at home before you leave, just in case you have to do it on the road.

Why Broken Spokes?

Spokes fail for a variety of reasons.

Overstressed spokes: The wheel isn't properly built, so certain spokes are overstressed. This is where the beginner gets into trouble with a spoke wrench.

Light spokes: The spokes are too light for the service. If you weigh 200 pounds or you carry touring loads, don't try to use 15- or 16-gauge, double-butted spokes. If you find your freewheel-side spokes breaking regularly, settle for plain 14-gauge spokes and accept the tiny weight penalty.

Defective spokes: This seems to be a problem with the cheapest spokes and with expensive, stainless steel spokes. I've stopped using such spokes.

Wheel construction: The wheel construction is wrong for the service. This is less important than the above reasons. Four-cross, low-flange wheels are less prone to spoke failures than the more normal three-cross, high-flange construction.

Frank Berto

How to Overhaul Your Cottered Crank

Michael A. Rosen

Ignore the rumors and innuendos. The three-piece cottered crank is a fine machine which has served many generations well. You might not know that it was used for racing until the last 10 or 15 years.

When the cottered crank is properly adjusted, it is as free spinning as an expensive sealed bearing. Because of its design and steel composition, this type of crank is comparatively rigid—a definite advantage.

Also, steel cranks usually have a narrower profile against the wind than those made of alloys. They are much less expensive and usually stronger. The disadvantages of this type of crank are not considered very important by many people: they are heavier than alloys, and they are a little more difficult to understand the mechanics and care of than your cotterless crank.

The first thing you need is a 4 × 4 about 11 inches long. You can either drill a hole near the edge of one end or saw a notch across one end (see figure 19), so that you can support the crank as you hammer the cotter. Thus the hammering force doesn't go into the bearings, which could cause damage.

Figure 19: How to prepare your crank for overhaul.

Loosen the cotter nut to the point of being flush with the outer end of the cotter pin, so you'll have a large, even surface on which to hammer (see figure 19). It is the force of this little pin wedged between the axle and the crankarm which keeps the crank rigidly attached to the axle, and which transmits the push/pull of pedaling into the turning of the wheel that propels the rider down the road. This pin is the Achilles' heel of this design. It is a small amount of metal to transmit such an amount of force. It is, however, plenty of metal to bear such force when properly maintained.

With this in mind, supporting the crank as in figure 19 with the 4 × 4, and using a drift punch, hammer gently on the nut so as not to damage the threads of the cotter (see figures 19 and 20). Hammer as long as necessary until the cotter loosens. Another way is to support the crank the same way on a vise opened to ½ inch. It is helpful, some say necessary, to have a friend hold the bike while you hammer. The wheels must be off the ground.

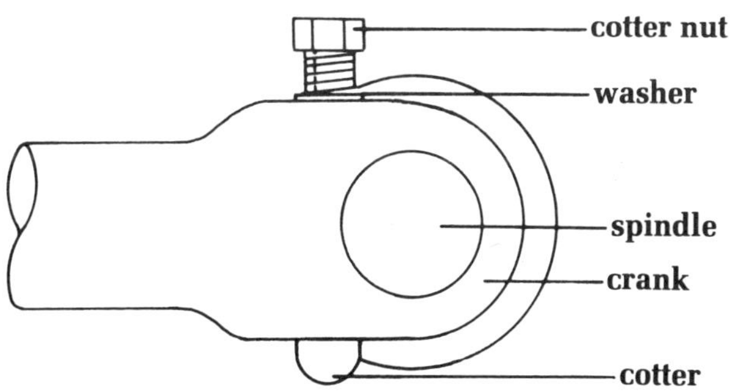

Figure 20: Sideview of cottered crank assembly.

Remove the nut. Drive the cotter the rest of the way out.

Various designs of bottom bracket locknuts exist, each with its own special tool. Many can be opened with a drift punch, hammer, and patience. The left side of the bottom bracket (which is what you want to take apart next) has left-hand threads if it has English threading (most common), or right-hand threads if it has Italian threading. Remove the cone after the locknut. Be prepared to catch the ball bearings.

Now, clean and inspect the entire contents of the bottom bracket. Replace parts as necessary. Another advantage of this type of project is the availability of parts for three-piece cranks.

When reassembling, reverse the procedure. Pack the bearings with clean bicycle grease. When replacing cotters, support the crank with a 4 × 4 section as before and hammer, using a drift punch against the unthreaded end ot the cotter, to proper tightness. Then tighten the cotter nut, but be careful not to strip the threads. All the tightness is gained by hammering, while the threads are only suitable to hold this tension. The threads will strip before you can get the cotter nut tight enough with a wrench to withstand the vibration to which this joint will be subjected.

After any removal, the cotter pin should be hammered (supported underneath by a 4 × 4) and the nut tightened every 50 miles for the next 250 miles. There is enough deformation in the steel to render this care necessary in tightening cotters. After this 250-mile treatment, cotters can be expected to stay tight.

Cotters come in different sizes. The differences (½ millimeter at a time) are invisible to the naked eye. Bring your old cotter to the shop (or, at the very least, be prepared to cite the brand name and country of origin of your bike) when you buy new cotters.

Head Bearing Maintenance

Chuck Harris

Head bearings contribute directly to the overall handling stability of the bicycle. Looseness here means every small riding jolt is accompanied with an audible knock. Binding can lead to shimmying at high speed, as well as general bad handling. Even more influential upon stability is the condition of the fork. Should it be bent backward or out of line or have a rake intended for a different frame head angle, steering may either over- or under-respond.

The lower head bearing takes the brunt of all road shocks and is considered by many to be poorly designed for this combined loading. It fails by dimpling and corrosion. The latter is due to the exposure to debris from the front brake and the relative inaccessibility of this bearing for routine cleaning without dismantling. Here is one instance where a ball retainer is decidedly ill-advised, as the load per ball is nearly double that of a loose-ball race.

The headset condition can be checked by first locking the front brake and rocking the bicycle back and forth. Feel both bearings for knock and listen for any head noise while rocking. Any noise means looseness. A finger placed directly on each cup while rocking will reveal any loose-fitting cups, which also produce play.

Pick up the front wheel and toss it from side (but don't slam it to avoid damage to the front brake). Any resistance to turning means binding. Uneven tightness means a deteriorated bearing or possibly a bent fork tube. This is one cause of "speed shimmy."

Head play is adjusted by loosening the locknut (and head clip, if used) and turning the upper race to tighten or loosen loading as required. Usually this race will turn freely by hand. Carefully check head performance after the locknut is retightened. If binding, cogging, or looseness persist after adjustment, dismantling is next.

In a typical headset structure, the bottom race, which may be a flat trough or a cone, is press-fitted onto a special seating at the base of the fork tube.

The bottom cup is press-fitted into the head tube, and sometimes may contain a loose-fitting balltrack. The race may use about 23 5/32-inch loose balls, or a greater number of 1/8-inch balls. If a ball retainer is found here, it should be replaced with a full complement of loose balls of the same size. The top cup is press-fitted into the head tube, and again may contain a removable balltrack. A ball retainer is permissible here but doesn't really make much sense.

The adjustable race is threaded onto the fork tube. Above it is a locking device keyed to a vertical slot in the tube. This might be a simple lockring, headlamp bracket, brake cable support, or a serrated lockring. Atop the locking device is a domed locknut. This may have either wrench faces or spanner holes.

Quite independent of the steering is the handlebar stem assembly. It is secured entirely within the fork tube by means of an expanding plunger, sliding wedge, or the now infrequently used head clip. The handlebar itself is secured in the stem by a clamp bolt or, in some roadster or juvenile machines, is permanently attached.

Steering head disassembly calls for release of both cables from their handlebar levers and of any light wiring. The handlebar stem is then removed by loosening the plunger bolt a few turns and tapping it into the stem with a padded hammer. On the road, use a stone covered by a cyclist's glove. The stem should loosen and the bolt should feel free after the tap. Catch the front wheel between the knees, twist the bars, and pull upward to remove the stem. The head-clip stem is removed simply by loosening the head-clip bolt.

Next, remove the locknut and lockring and then remove the front wheel. Lay the bicycle on its side and prepare to catch the loose ball bearings from each race as the adjustable race is removed, either by hand or wrench. Pull the fork out of the frame and inspect top and bottom cups and bottom race for a tight fit.

After cleaning, check all races for pitting or dimpling, and replace any worn or corroded parts. The bottom race should fit snugly on its fork-tube seat. Looseness here with a new part requires either another race, careful and expert shimming, or even building up the seat by torch. Loose top and bottom cups are best replaced while shimming can correct looseness in a new part. Dimpling with a punch is not permanent and not advised here.

Defective cups are driven out of the head tube by means of a stick and hammer. Because of the normally tight fit, each tap will withdraw the cup only slightly and pressure will have to be applied along the entire inside circumference. Cups are installed by tapping them into place with a hammer and board. Be sure they are fully seated before assembling the head.

Grease is a satisfactory lubricant for head bearings and takes little energy to apply. Turn the bicycle upside down and fill the bottom cup with balls, pressing them into the greased track. Then drop the fork carefully into position. Grease the adjustable race and fill it with balls and then carefully thread it upward until it pulls the head together snugly. The remaining parts—lockring, accessories, locknut, and head clip, if used—are then put together, the front wheel is installed, and the handlebar stem reinserted.

Expander or sliding wedges are installed loosely and the stem is inserted at least 2 inches into the fork tube. This is critical because the presence of the expander within the fork-tube threads can easily start a crack and separation of the threaded portion of the fork tube that will release the handlebars and possibly drop the fork. I would like to mention at this point that some inexpensive Japanese "replacement" forks are threaded down almost the entire length of the head tube, leaving the fork vulnerable to thread splitting, no matter how the stem is installed.

The handlebar is lined up to the front wheel by eye and the expander bolt tightened. A head clip cannot be tightened until head play is adjusted. Check head play as described earlier, using the front brake, and adjust the loose race. Tighten down the locknut and again check for freedom from knock. Loosen the locknut to make any fine corrections. Finally, tighten the locknut well and check the handlebar clamp in the stem by bearing down upon the handlebar ends. Looseness here is annoying since a sudden road jolt can result in an abrupt change of handlebar position.

General Bearing Maintenance

Chuck Harris

Bicycle ball-bearing assemblies—hubs, pedals, headsets, derailleur idlers, and bottom brackets—are all subject to wear. They generally aren't sealed and require periodic lubrication.

After bad weather or extended disuse, a bearing may freeze up and fail to roll freely, even after being soaked with penetrating oil. It may become grit-infested and intolerably noisy.

Curiously, new bicycles often arrive with the bracket and hub bearings virtually locked—a condition which will wreck a precision-bearing race in a few miles.

Often bearings are packed with grease. A greased pedal won't spin, and a bottom bracket with grease won't spin with the chain off. Greased wheels are sluggish, but the presence of grease is harder to detect. It may show oozing from the bearings of a new hub.

The following notes cover the dismantling and reassembly of hub, pedal, and derailleur idler bearings.

Front and rear hubs are similar in construction (exceptions being rear gear hubs, coaster brakes, and centrifugal clutch-type freewheels). A useful adjustment tool is a flat cone wrench. A pair of tweezers is useful for ball insertion. Hubs are dismantled by removing the wheel nuts or quick-release spindle, and removing one cone locknut by gripping the opposite side. Pull off the keyed lockwasher and unscrew the cone. Tip the wheel and catch the balls or retainer that may fall out. Pick them out if embedded in grease or grit. Pull out the axle and catch the bearings from the opposite side. Clean and inspect cones, balls, and hub races for rust or pitting. Check the axle for bending and damaged threads. Due to variations of thread, body diameter, length, radius, and several other variables, it is almost mandatory to replace cones of the same manufacture as the hub. Almost any solvent is suitable for cleaning bearings.

Pedals are dismantled by first removing the cap (commonly, the relatively smooth cap surface requires pliers for a positive grip), and loosening the bearing locknut. Now remove the pedal from the crank, observing the correct direction, depending on the side of the bicycle to which it belongs. Remove the bearing locknut and pull out the lockwasher. Unscrew the cone and tip out the top balls. Now pull out the spindle and catch the inside balls. Cones, races, and balls are again inspected for damage after cleaning. Scraping of the spindle by the pedal shell can be caused by loose bearing adjustment or a hopelessly worn and undercut spindle cone.

Derailleur idlers are best cleaned by dismantling if they cannot be freed by penetrating oil in position. Most parallelogram derailleurs allow easy idler removal by means of separate bolts.

Plastic sleeve bearing idlers aren't trouble-free by any means. Grit can gall the inside bearing surface or the sleeve surface can rust, causing binding. Grit can cause an oversize hole. A galled hole must be filed clean, and rust sanded off the sleeve.

Ball-bearing idlers are dismantled by unscrewing the cone assembly and catching the balls. Only a deeply gouged cone is likely to indicate replacement. The slight drag introduced by a pitted cone is probably negligible.

The idler is reassembled by placing the longer cone face up and dropping the idler body over it. A drop of light motor oil is placed in the balltrack, and the balls are dropped, one by one, into the track. After a few are inserted, pick up the idler a fraction of an inch, and the balls will fall outward into place in their track. Enough balls are inserted so that there is a gap of about one ball-width remaining. The small cone is then threaded onto the stem of the long cone and tightened to binding and then backed about one quarter-turn. After reinstallation, the cone is fine-adjusted (with a small screwdriver or other point) until there is slight play after the mounting bolt is tightened.

The pedal is reassembled by supporting the body with the inside bearing up, the spindle dropped loosely in place, and balls dropped singly into the gap as the spindle is picked up slightly. A few drops of oil are placed on the track. After a few balls are inserted, the spindle is dropped to position the balls outward, and the number checked. Again, sufficient balls are inserted to fill the track with a gap of about one. Now the pedal is flipped over, with the loose spindle carefully supported. Prop the pedal upright by its spindle (a vise is best), and drop a few balls into the oiled upper track.

The cone is threaded onto the spindle, and in far enough to check the number of balls still required in the upper race. It is then backed up far enough to insert the remaining balls. Then it is threaded down to the point of binding, and backed slightly. If too many balls are accidentally inserted, the pedal won't turn very freely, and the cone will clearly be off-center as the pedal is turned. The lockwasher is dropped into place atop the correctly adjusted cone, and the locknut threaded into position.

The cone is adjusted (the slots protrude slightly beyond the width of the lockwasher to facilitate this), and the locknut trial-tightened. When the pedal spins freely with barely perceptible play, adjustment is optimum. A worn spindle will require greater play as the spindle bearing wears out of round. The locknut is driven tightly home when adjustment is complete; a loose locknut allows the cone to wind up tightly and suddenly when in use and results in a locked pedal. Add a few drops of oil to the outer bearing and reinstall the dust cap snugly.

Hubs are reassembled by first installing or leaving one cone and locknut in position on the spindle, and dropping the spindle down into the hub. Balls are dropped into this side after adding a drop of oil. The spindle is picked up to allow ball entry, and dropped back into position to check the ball placement in the track. Here, as elsewhere, a slight gap is desired between balls when the race is properly filled. The wheel is then picked up, flipped, and then supported by its spindle (best in a vise). Balls are now inserted on the opposite side, and the cone threaded onto the spindle to check progress, and backed off to admit additional balls.

When full, the cone is hand-threaded home, the lockwasher dropped on, and the locknut threaded on. Play can easily be adjusted with the wheel still in the vise or back in place in the bicycle frame. The locknut is loosened slightly, the cone adjusted with the cone wrench for minimal play, and the locknut tightened. Slight play should remain after the locknut is finally tightened.

Wheel and Bracket Bearing Adjustment

Fred DeLong

The frames built in bicycle production consist of relatively flexible members, subject to heavy impact loads that result in bending under operating conditions. The stresses from heating and cooling during joining of lugs, tubes, and fork end result in slight misalignments. Unless the built-in cooling stresses are relieved, and the bearing and axle seats are aligned or machined to precise accuracy after building, a perfect bearing seat cannot be expected. Even if perfect, misalignment from mishandling or from operating stress can still ensue.

It is for this reason that successful precision bearing components rely on a design involving considerable rigidity, and that conventional bicycle bearings are made with "cup and cone" construction. The ball contact is at an angle with the axle, rather than perpendicular to it, and this angle is opposed at the two ends. Thus, loads from all directions can be accommodated by the two bearings. Radius of cup or cone bearing surface is large in comparison to ball radius, which permits the inaccuracies of shell, axle, or cone to be accommodated along the extended ball path. End adjustment of one of the members takes up slack in the bearings, so that a smooth-running assembly, free of undesirable play and wobble, will result. Of course, an axle bent or cup misaligned beyond the limits of design will cause excessive loading at one point on the bearing. This will result in premature failure, but in a wheel bearing, the cone can be turned by rotating the axle so that an undamaged portion supports the major applied load. I've known this technique to work sufficiently well to permit completion of a week-long tour in an area where no spare parts were available. A little study of weight and drive train load components will enable you to decide the exact position to place the damaged bearing surface.

Many neophyte mechanics wonder after setting the bearing adjustment, why it seems to change when "locking up" the adjustment. An excellent play-free, easy-spinning adjustment suddenly becomes too tight. Then if made intentionally loose, it stays loose upon insertion of the wheel in the frame or tightening the bracket lockring. Actually, each adjustment is an individual case, although skill and experience is a factor.

Consider again manufacturing tolerances. Threaded parts must have a certain looseness of fit to permit ease of assembly. With threads triangular in shape, this clearance in a vertical direction (perpendicular to the axle) also permits horizontal play to exist.

Now, to prevent the adjusted cone member from rotation on the axle from the friction of the balls when under load, a locknut is used. This is tightened against the cone, and friction between it and the cone prevents each from further rotation (unless friction between the balls and cone is great because of dirty bearings or chipped ball races).

But if the cone is properly adjusted before tightening the locknut, the tightening of the locknut will press the cone inward part or all of the axial clearance between the threads. Thus the initial hand adjustment is made tighter, and binding of the bearings may result. Since the amount of clearance between individual axles and cones can vary, and since accuracy of bearing surfaces also varies, this tightening effect is not uniform in every assembly.

The amount of pressure that can be applied to a bearing assembly can be very great. Chain plus pedal pressure load on a bottom bracket axle bearing may run 500 to 700 pounds; on the rear hub, chain pull plus weight load runs a somewhat similar amount; front hub bearing load may run 60 to 100 pounds, split between the two bearings.

Tighten the bearing adjustment with a 4-inch wrench, using a force of only 4 pounds, and consider a 1-millimeter thread pitch, and an extra tightening of only one-quarter turn on the cone (the minimum adjustment on a Sturmey-Archer rear hub, for example). The cone would screw in about $^{1}/_{100}$ inch. Accounting for half the wrench force lost in friction, an end loading of 1,250 can result. But due to the angle of contact of balls and bearing surface, this end force is multiplied (the amount depends on bearing design) so that an actual load of 2,500 pounds can easily be generated! Thus the working load on the bearing can greatly be exceeded, and bearing life shortened and friction increased.

Fitting and Repairing Cables

Chuck Harris

This series of sketches illustrates some points on the fitting, repair, servicing, and selection of cables for brakes and gearshifts.

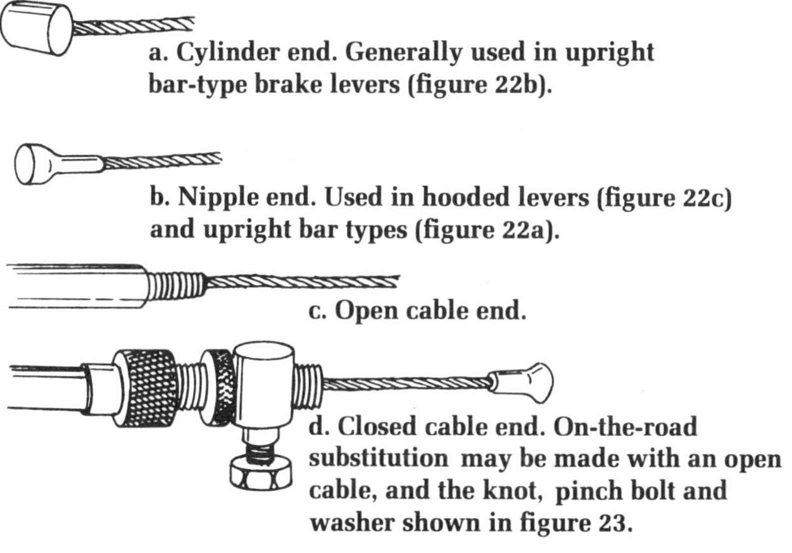

Figure 21: Cable end types.

Figure 21 shows the most frequently encountered cable end types. The closed-end cable (that is, nipple at both ends) offers simpler assembly to inexperienced persons. Unfortunately, due to its high replacement cost, poor interchangeability, and the impossibility of reaching its inner portions for inspection and cleaning, it is not the preferred type for serious cyclists.

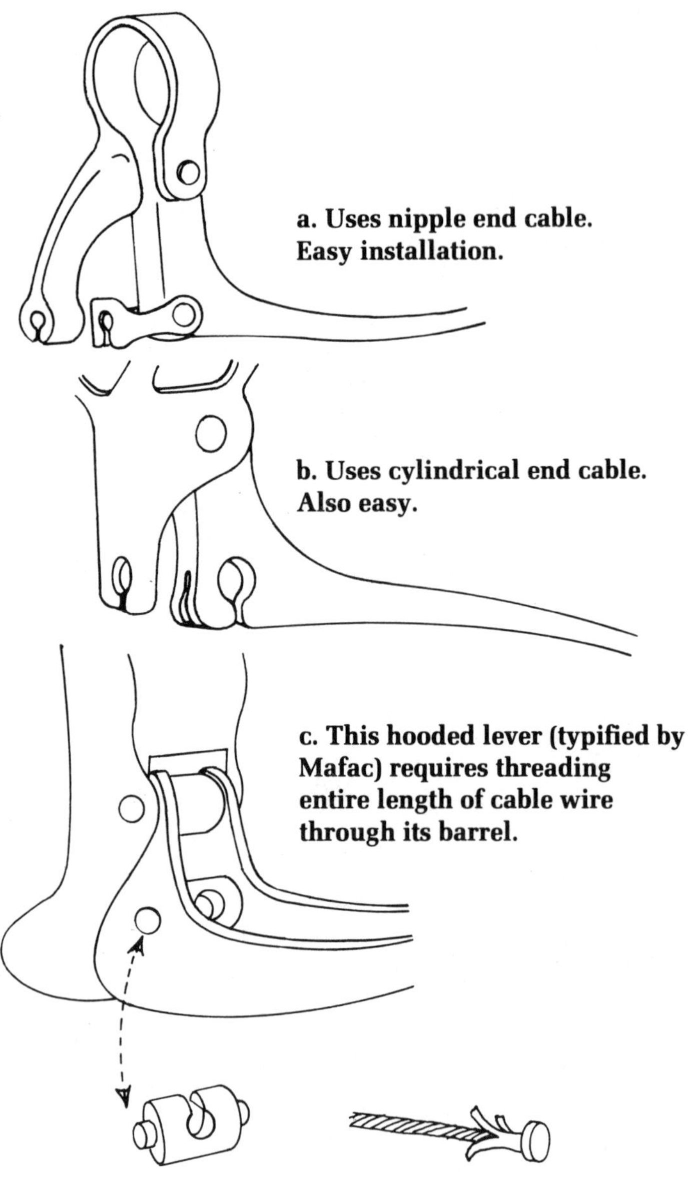

d. Some hooded levers use a split barrel and hood for ease of installation. However, the cable nipple can fail as shown on this type more frequently than breaking. Field-repair with nipple shown in figure 23 if exact replacement isn't on hand.

Figure 22: Fitting of cable end in brake levers.

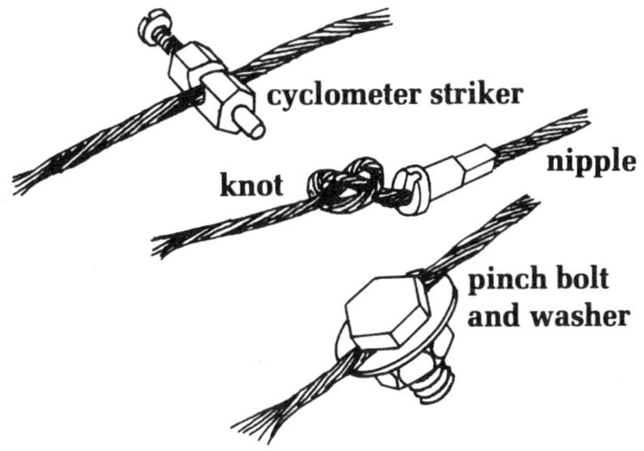

Figure 23: Several on-the-road end repair methods.

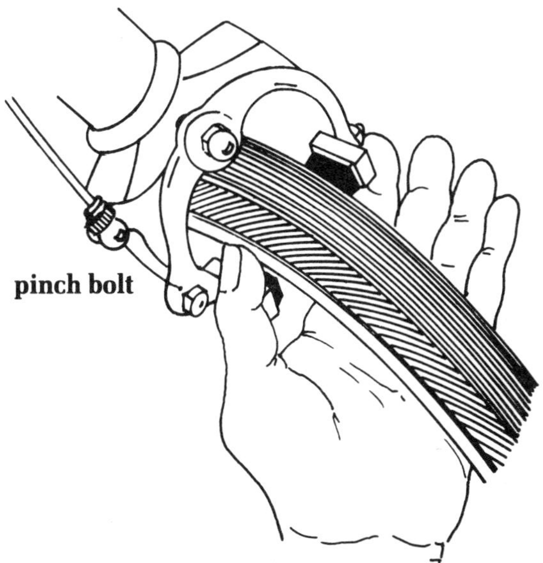

Figure 24: Open-end cable installation: first, be sure cable is properly seated in lever, and that adjuster is seated to about ⅛ inch. Squeeze brake against rim as shown, and with other hand, pull cable tight through pinch bolt and finger-tighten it. Then finish tightening bolt properly after removing hand. Check lever operation with full force.

Figure 22 shows brake lever cable seats. Among hooded levers, the completely closed-entry Mafac type is safer than the split-entry of Figure 21d, despite the more cumbersome cable insertion procedure of the former.

Figure 23 stresses that a broken cable on the road is no reason to ride with one less brake or without the ability to shift gears. Even a too-short cable can be used if its housing is shortened or something is tied within an open run in order to lengthen it sufficiently to allow for the knot or other improvised end.

Figure 24 illustrates installation of the loose end of an open-end cable in the brake pinch-bolt. Admittedly, this is still not easy for the novice.

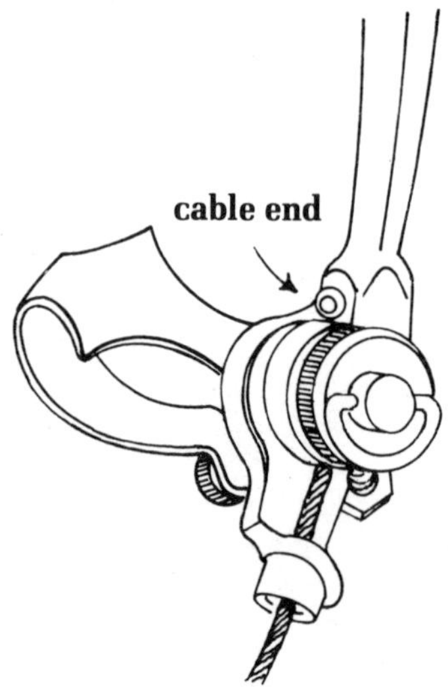

Figure 25: This type of gear lever has an open-cable seat. The cable is easily replaced, and emergency substitution of a brake cable or a knotted end is easy.

Figures 25 and 26 show two typical gear levers and point out the cable seatings.

Figure 27 shows a cable guide for the rear derailleur cable where it passes the bottom bracket. Some bicycles use either a fully enclosed cable or a segment of housing for this run. Either one is vulnerable to the inevitable splash from both wheels, and a cable housing is a natural water and grit trap. The open guide is easily cleaned.

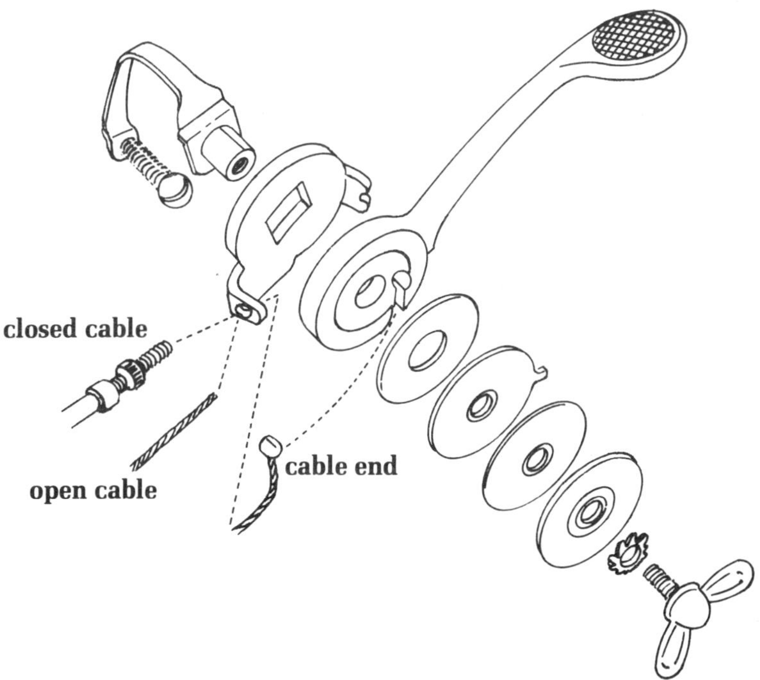

Figure 26: This type of gear lever (Huret and early Simplex) must be dismantled to replace the cable. In an emergency, a tight knot at the end of any cable will replace the ball or cylindrical end of the original cable. Frequently inspect visible portion of the cable where it bends around the lever as a little rust or a broken strand here means a full break is imminent.

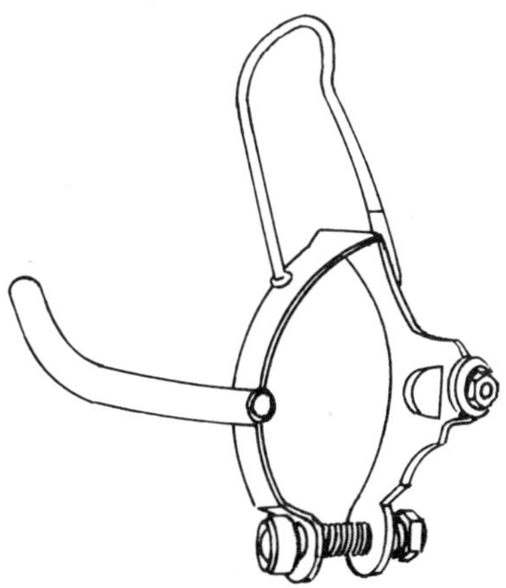

Figure 27: Typical guide for open-gear cable run by bottom bracket. Unlike cable housing used at this point, the guide is not likely to freeze solid suddenly or pack up with grit.

A Timetable for the Care of Your Bicycle

	EVERY RIDE	EVERY MONTH
HEADSET	*Be careful in cleaning not to shove dirt further into moving parts.*	Check for looseness, if you haven't noticed it already riding. (Pick up bike by handlebars and shake.)
DERAILLEUR	Clean with soft cloth and toothbrush.	Oil Simplex and Huret shift levers. (Oil Campy or shifter with ratchets every 3 months.)
BRAKES	Be sure both wheels skid when bike is pushed with brakes applied. Check cables for fraying. Do pads hit rim properly?	CENTERPULL—Oil stirrup cable pivot and stirrup hanger. SIDEPULL—Oil between brake arms and washers on either end (all parts of center bolt that rub one another).
WHEELS, HUBS AND TIRES	Is hub tight? Are wheels true? Are they centered on the frame? Clean with soft cloth and toothbrush. Are valves straight? A slanted valve could mean a slow leak. Check for cuts, wear, or bulges.	Check rack and fender mounting bolts.
CRANK AND CHAIN	Clean with soft cloth and toothbrush.	*Apply the smallest amount of oil possible.*
PEDALS	Clean with soft cloth and toothbrush.	*There are over 230 ball bearings in a bicycle. Each one should be cleaned and lubricated at least once a year.*
MISCELLANEOUS	*Use a silicone or petroleum oil, NEVER 3-in-1 or any other vegetable-based oil. It gums the works.*	Gently scrape off accumulated grease on chainwheel teeth with screwdriver.

This timetable assumes an average riding frequency of at least four rides a week and a minimum distance of 40 miles a month. However, bicyclists who only ride once a month should pay much closer attention to "Every Ride" care. Notes in italics apply to all components. If you ride on dusty roads, in wet weather, or ride a lot, the "Once a Year" chores should be done every six months.

EVERY 3 MONTHS	EVERY 6 MONTHS	ONCE A YEAR
Check for grittiness in turning the bars (sort of a sandy feel).		Disassemble, replace worn bearings, lubricate, and rebuild.*
Oil all rubbing parts. Oil other derailleur types (see "Every Month"). Grease or oil cables.		Replace cables.
Check for wear on brake pads. Grease or oil cables.	*Never oil any part of a bicycle unless it is spotlessly clean.*	Replace cables.
Check for grittiness. Freewheel wobble is a natural phenomenon due to the way it is set on the hub. Don't worry about that—just keep it clean.	If you've had no flats in 6 months, reglue your sew-up tires.	Disassemble, replace worn bearings, lubricate, and rebuild.* Check your spokes. Have any corroded?
Oil all rubbing parts. A tick or jerkiness in the turning of a cottered crank probably means a loose cotter pin.	Is your chain stretched? (Does it pull away from the teeth more than half the length of a tooth in high gear?) Oil chain if it squeaks or has any rust.	Disassemble, replace worn bearings, lubricate, and rebuild.*
There are over 80 nuts and bolts on a bicycle. Each should be checked for tightness and lubricated if it is a pivot point. Threads should be kept spotlessly clean.	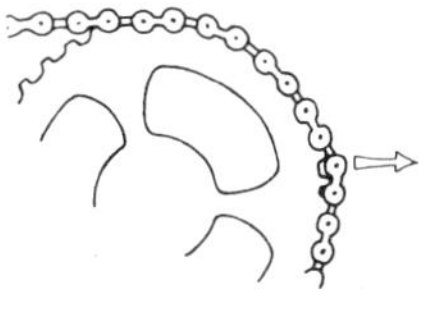	Disassemble, replace worn bearings, lubricate, and rebuild.* (Note: Some pedals come with bearings and some with plastic rings. Those without removable dust caps cannot be replaced. Just run with them until they wear out.)
Treat your leather saddle.	Check for rust between stem and fork steerer and grease if necessary. (Electrolyte action may weld these together. Sweat makes them worse. Those who use rollers and sweat, take note.)	**Do these at the bike shop, unless you have invested in the special tools required.*